ESRI

THE ECONOMIC AND SOCIAL RESEARCH INSTITUTE

The Economic and Social Research Institute (ESRI) is a non-profit organisation which was founded in 1960 as The Economic Research Institute. The Institute is a private company, limited by guarantee, and enjoys full academic independence. It is governed by a Council consisting of 32 members who are representative of business, trade unions, government departments, state agencies, universities and other research institutes.

GUIDANCE FOR ALL?

Guidance Provision in Second-Level Schools

Selina McCoy
Emer Smyth
Merike Darmody
Allison Dunne

The Liffey Press
in association with
The Economic and Social Research Institute

the
liffey
press

Published by
The Liffey Press
Ashbrook House
10 Main Street
Raheny, Dublin 5, Ireland
www.theliffeypress.com

© 2006 The Economic and Social Research Institute

A catalogue record of this book is
available from the British Library.

ISBN 1-905785-03-8

Printed in Ireland by ColourBooks Ltd.

CONTENTS

LIST OF TABLES AND FIGURES

List of Tables

List of Figures

ACKNOWLEDGEMENTS

This study was commissioned by the Department of Education and Science. We are very grateful to Maureen Bohan and her colleagues for their unfailing support and advice.

The study would not have been possible without the assistance of school principals, guidance counsellors and students. In particular, we would like to express our sincere gratitude to the staff and students of the fifteen case study schools for giving generously of their time.

Within the ESRI, we would like to thank our colleagues Brendan Whelan, Philip O'Connell, Anne Nolan and Nicola Doyle for helpful comments on earlier drafts of the study. The staff of the survey unit were, as always, professional and diligent in their work. We are especially grateful to James Williams. Finally, Pat Hopkins is to be thanked for her efficient production of copies of the versions of the book.

Any remaining errors and omissions are the sole responsibility of the authors.

Chapter One

INTRODUCTION

1.1 INTRODUCTION

In recent years, reviews of guidance have been undertaken by various international organisations, including the OECD, CEDEFOP and the World Bank. These reviews attempt to place guidance in a broader, life-long perspective addressing issues such as the contribution of guidance to improving the efficiency of the education system; its role in promoting a tighter link between education and work; its role in supporting labour market and economic goals; and its contribution to helping to attain social equity and inclusion. The reviews reflect the growing interest in guidance issues across a range of settings and groups of people, including students in second-level schools. However, relatively little attention has focused on the counselling or personal/social support dimension of guidance provision, particularly within the school context. Rather, most international attention has been focused on the *career* guidance aspect of the role, partly reflecting the diverse definitions of guidance and the differing functions it serves across societies. This study sets out to address this gap in research for the Irish context and provides a comprehensive examination of the nature, function and operation of Guidance Counselling services in Irish second-level schools.

In general, guidance is defined in various ways across Europe (see Sultana, 2004). However, essentially ". . . the term is used to refer to a set of interrelated activities that have, as a goal, the structured provision of information and assistance to enable individuals and groups, of any age and at any point throughout their lives, to make choices on educational, training, and occupational trajectories and to manage their life paths effectively" (p. 24). While this definition is useful, it lacks the dimension of personal and social support to assist people in coping with the changes taking place in society.

Countries use different terminology to refer to the persons providing guidance. Sultana (2004) suggests that different terminology may signal different approaches to guidance. For example, in the education sector several countries use the term "Guidance Counsellors" (Flemish-speaking Belgium, France, Greece, Iceland, as well as Ireland – see Sultana, 2004, p. 27). In the Irish context, the National Centre for Guidance in Education (NCGE, 2004) defines guidance in schools as ". . . a range of learning experiences provided in a developmental sequence that assist students to make choices (personal and social, educational and career) about their lives and to make transitions consequent on these choices" (p. 8). In other words, the term characterises the complex role Guidance Counsellors have in Irish schools.[1]

This study examines Guidance Counselling provision in Irish second-level schools. Previous studies within the Irish context have attempted to look at specific aspects of guidance provision in second-level schools. Regular audits of Guidance Counsellors, undertaken by the NCGE, monitor the allocation of guidance time in schools and the resources available for guidance. A survey of members of the Institute of Guidance Counsellors (IGC) was undertaken in 2003, which detailed the key activities of Guidance Counsellors in schools. In addition, a number of studies have examined specific aspects of the role of Guidance Counsellors (Shiel and Lewis, 1993; Hannan *et al.*, 1983, for example). These and other studies, however, identify a gap in understanding about the precise role of Guidance Counsellors in Irish schools and a lack of information about the delivery of guidance services within schools. As Hannan *et al.* commented in 1983, there is a lack of data available on the specific content of guidance and counselling programmes or on the ways in which Guidance Counsellors present information to students. This lack of knowledge does not appear to have improved in the intervening period. In addition, earlier studies have identified a need for an examination of students' satisfaction with their guidance experiences with a view

---

[1] It is important to note that "counselling" in this context does not generally refer to a specialised therapeutic function, but rather to personal and social support.

to determining how students felt those experiences had helped them in making personal, educational and career decisions.

The Economic and Social Research Institute (ESRI), commissioned by the Department of Education and Science, set out to undertake a comprehensive examination of the nature of Guidance Counselling provision in second-level schools across the country. The study complements, and contributes to, the review of guidance provision being undertaken by the NCGE and Department of Education and Science. The study comprised two phases: phase one involved a postal survey of Principals, Guidance Counsellors and personnel with guidance hours in 260 second-level schools. The survey focused on collecting detailed information on guidance provision within schools from the perspective of the main personnel involved. It covered topics such as the level of guidance provision in schools, the amount of time devoted to the provision of guidance, the types of guidance activities being undertaken and the facilities provided for the delivery of guidance. Information collected as part of the postal survey was used to identify schools with varying levels and types of guidance provision. These schools formed the focus for in-depth case-study research in phase two of the study.

Further details on the background of the study and the methodology employed are presented in Sections 1.5 and 1.6. The following sections consider the context of the Guidance Counselling service in Irish second-level schools, discussing the historical background, current policy provision and the international context.

1.2 LITERATURE REVIEW

1.2.1 Guidance at second level: The historical background

A guidance and counselling service was formally established in Irish second-level schools by the Department of Education in 1966. The establishment of this service was attributed to a response to the needs created by wider processes of rapid industrialisation that took place in Ireland during the 1960s, a slowing down in emigration and the availability of a wider range of careers for young people (Shiel and Lewis, 1993). The Shiel and Lewis report also suggested that provision was at a relatively high level by international standards until 1983; up to that year, a full-time ex-quota Guidance Counsellor was allocated to schools with more than 250 students. In 1983 this threshold was raised to 500; below that level no provision was made. In 1991 a more graduated approach was introduced with a half ex-quota post allocated to schools in the 350-499 enrolment category. Research by the Institute of Guidance Counsellors (IGC, 1990) indicated considerable variation in provision across school types – 5 per cent of community/comprehensive, 18 per cent of secondary and 34 per cent of vocational schools offered no guidance service to their students. Similarly, McCarthy (1993) pointed to the need for greater provision in vocational schools and schools in rural areas where total enrolment is often less than 350 students.

Over the years, the importance of Guidance Counselling services in schools has been highlighted in various policy reports and government documents focusing on the nature of the service. The Green Paper on Education (1992) defines guidance in schools as broadly ". . . all the services, programmes and activities within a school which are aimed at helping students to achieve an understanding of themselves and their potential". The paper also stipulates that ". . . the school works with parents to help their children to develop positive attitudes and behaviour and to make satisfying and fulfilling educational and career choices" (ibid., p. 107). Importantly, in addition to involving parents in this process, the report perceives the service as a "school-wide responsibility", as well as an "ongoing and developmental" activity which should address the following areas:

1. Appraisal and assessment – in order to ". . . enable the school to understand the needs of the student, as well as helping students and their parents to understand themselves better";

2. Information – in order to "enable students to make informed decisions about educational, vocational and career choices"; and

3. Counselling, a service ". . . which would be available to all students, but particularly to those experiencing learning or personal difficulties and those in special situations in the school, such as those from disadvantaged communities or those with disabilities, potential

early-school leavers and students at significant transition points within their school careers" (p. 107).

The Report of the National Education Convention (Coolahan, 1994) addressed a number of issues relating to guidance provision in schools. In general, the report called for greater emphasis on educational guidance at both levels of second-level education, that is, junior and senior cycle, as well as the need for greater availability of psychological services and greater integration of the work of psychologists and teachers (p. 66). Some guidance-related issues were also included in the White Paper on Education (1995) mostly referring back to the Convention recommendations.

The Education Act introduced in 1998 stipulated the provision of guidance as a statutory requirement in schools that should ". . . ensure that students have access to appropriate guidance to assist them in their educational and career choices" and "promote the moral, spiritual, social and personal development of students . . . in consultation with their parents, having regard to the characteristic spirit of the school" (section 9). However, what constitutes "appropriate guidance" was not discussed in the document. In fact, such vagueness in terms of guidelines for appropriate provision can lead to a wide variation among schools in the nature of their Guidance Counselling services, as argued by the NCGE in a later document (National Centre for Guidance in Education, 2001, pp. 47–48). The Act also recommends that all schools use a well-developed and comprehensive school plan. The NCGE (2004) suggests that such a plan ". . . should make specific reference to guidance and should incorporate a school guidance plan". Elsewhere guidance was seen as ". . . forming an integral component of the school development plan, with specific policy in this area being developed collaboratively by school management, guidance personnel and other staff involved in the provision of services in this area" (McGuinness, 2001. p. 75).

The function of the service is discussed also in the National Development Plan (1999):

> . . . [the] school Guidance Service, [. . .] has a major preventative role in helping young people at risk to remain in the formal education system. This service will be complemented by provision for guidance under the Lifelong Learning Measure for young people and

adults who have either failed within or been failed by the formal system. The provision of guidance and counselling in second level
schools is vital to enable each pupil to gain the maximum benefit from
the education system. The aims of the School Guidance Service are to
prevent difficulties encountered by students hindering their participation in, or benefiting from, the education system and to provide guidance regarding further education and third level options (p. 99).

The primary statutory agency with responsibility in this area, the NCGE
(2004), defines Guidance Counselling as a service which is provided
through the school guidance programme. This programme incorporates
". . . the specific set of learning experiences which a school provides in
response to the guidance needs of its students" (p. 8). The areas addressed by guidance services in schools can be divided into three inter-
linked areas: 1) personal and social; 2) educational; and 3) career. The
main guidance activities within these areas include: a) counselling; b)
assessment; c) information; d) advice; e) Educational Development Programmes; f) Personal and Social Development Programmes; and g) referral (p. 12). In general, guidance in schools is seen as a ". . . whole
school responsibility involving the provision of advice and support to all
students on a continuous basis, especially to those experiencing difficulty and at risk of early school leaving" (McGuinness, 2001, p. 75). It
should be noted, however, that while the official publications discuss
Guidance Counselling provision in certain specific areas, in practice,
". . . the emphasis given to each of these activities is likely to vary depending on such factors as school ethos, the interests and preferences of
counsellors themselves, and the functions assigned to other teachers in
school" (Shiel and Lewis, 1993, p. 8).

1.3 CURRENT POLICY AND PROVISION

1.3.1 Aims, objectives and target groups

Vocational preparation, personal development and wider options have
been central themes in Guidance Counselling since its introduction into
Irish second-level schools in the 1960s (Jeffers, 2002). Such a broad, and
largely discretionary, role remains a central feature of guidance policy
today, over 40 years after its introduction. While the Department of Edu-

cation and Science (henceforth the Department) sets out guidelines for schools for the provision of guidance services to students and allocates resources, schools have considerable discretion regarding the exact nature of the guidance services offered to their students.

Despite its broad nature, the provision of guidance is a statutory requirement for second-level schools under the Education Act (1998). According to Department Guidelines (2005), the school guidance programme should reflect the needs of both junior and senior cycle students, and should provide a balance between the personal, social, educational and career guidance offered. It identifies the main aim of guidance as an ongoing process involving a wide range of learning activities, such as information giving, counselling and assessment. Schools are required to provide "appropriate guidance" to all students – this includes providing students with:

- Clear information concerning subject choices;

- An awareness of the subject content, the skills and competencies they may acquire, and the study demands of the subject;

- An opportunity to explore their interests and subject choices and how these link to career areas;

- Assistance in the choice of educational programmes offered by the school (JCSP, TY, LCA, LCVP);

- Assistance in identifying their own most effective learning styles and in developing effective study and note-taking skills, examination techniques and time management skills;

- Guidance on educational, vocational and career options available; and

- Encouragement to explore a wide range of educational and career choices including non-traditional careers (Department of Education and Science, 2005).

Allied to the guidance role of schools, the Department (DES) also offers guidelines to schools in the domain of personal and social education.

They identify a particular contribution of guidance to personal and social education in enabling students to (among others):

- Recognise their own talents and achievements, and identify their strengths and weaknesses;

- Develop coping strategies to deal with stress, personal and social issues, and the challenges posed by adolescence and adulthood;

- Develop interpersonal skills and awareness of the needs of others;

- Establish good patterns of decision making and learn how to make informed choices; and

- Make successful transitions from primary to post-primary and from post-primary to further or higher education, training or directly into employment (Department of Education and Science, 2005).

Finally, the Department (2005) suggests that school guidance pro-grammes can support a proactive inclusive school policy through the early identification and support of students at risk of early school leav-ing, guidance support for school attendance strategies and thorough awareness among students of the consequences of early school leaving. They also cite the importance of strategies for building motivation and self-esteem.

The Department considers guidance as a whole school responsibility which should involve the Guidance Counsellor, in the first instance, as well as all other relevant members of management and staff of the school. It also considers that guidance should be centrally involved in the transition from primary to second-level education, in progressing through junior cycle, during senior cycle and progression from senior cycle (Department of Education and Science, 2005).

The limited research which has been undertaken shows considerable variation in the provision and utilisation of guidance services in Irish schools. The main personnel in schools providing the guidance services are Guidance Counsellors in conjunction with other personnel. Jeffers (2002) argues that role definitions of Guidance Counsellors have been general in character and involve a number of different tasks. He explains that, in fact, ". . . in the early days many Guidance Counsellors actively resisted too much role clarification in order to highlight the need for flexibility so as to be able to respond appropriately to the varied needs of individual situations" (p. 6).

Earlier research has found that many of the Guidance Counselling activities in Irish schools are undertaken with senior cycle students. However, some guidance is provided in junior cycle in terms of subject choice (Hannan *et al.*, 1983; Shiel and Lewis, 1993) and all students are generally encouraged to approach Guidance Counsellors with personal issues.

Guidance Counsellors are ". . . generally recruited from the ranks of serving second-level teachers and must have at least three years of teaching experience" (Shiel and Lewis, 1993, p. 7). Each Guidance Counsellor is required to have a post-graduate diploma in guidance (one year full-time course) in addition to a teaching qualification (OECD, 2003, p. 42). However, having such members of personnel in schools with a specific qualification in guidance and counselling is relatively recent (Jeffers, 2002). Indeed, it is still possible to have "unqualified" people with guidance hours, an issue which is examined in this book.

In many cases, a person responsible for the delivery of guidance and counselling is also involved in teaching. Shiel and Lewis (1993) argue that "Counsellors who engage in more subject teaching have less time available for counselling in general, and personal counselling in particular than their counterparts who do not have a strong involvement in subject teaching". However, such diversity makes it difficult to develop guidelines for practice and has created tensions around timetabling as well as the Guidance Counsellor's role.

Agencies

The Department of Education and Science offers guidelines to schools to enable them to provide "appropriate guidance" for their students. Inspectors of Guidance are available to school management and staff to advise on all aspects of school guidance provision. The Department also sets out the resources available to schools for such purposes. It is supported by the NCGE.

The NCGE, an agency of the Department of Education and Science, was set up in 1995 to support and develop guidance practice in all areas of education and to inform the policy of the Department in the field of guidance. Among the main activities of the Centre are:

- Promoting and supporting strategies for the provision of guidance and counselling in the context of lifelong learning;

- Developing and evaluating guidance resources;

- Providing support for innovative guidance projects;

- Providing opportunities for in-career development for guidance practitioners;

- Promoting, developing and disseminating good practice in guidance.

The Institute of Guidance Counsellors (IGC), established in 1968, is the professional body representing over 1,000 guidance practitioners, predominantly operating in second-level schools. It has a liaison and advocacy role with government departments, trade union organisations, national parents' bodies, colleges of higher/further education and representatives of industry. It also sets standards for the practice of guidance and counselling and supports the professional development of its members through in-career training. According to recent commentary in the area, "The NCGE, along with the Institute of Guidance Counsellors (IGC), have been the most active players in shaping the role of the counsellor and in identifying boundaries" (Jeffers, 2003, p. 5).

Resources

The Department of Education and Science allocates guidance counselling hours to schools based on the total number of students enrolled. At the time of this research, allocations were determined on the following basis (the system of allocation for 2004/05, as detailed on the Department of Education and Science website in February 2005):

Table 1.1: Allocation of guidance hours: 2004/05 academic year

Recognised Pupil Enrolment	Allocation
1,000+	2 posts (44 hrs/wk)
800–999	1.5 posts (33 hrs/wk)
500–799	1 post (22 hrs/wk)
250–499	0.5 post (11 hrs/wk)
200–249	0.4 post (8.8 hrs/wk)
<200	0.36 post (8 hrs/wk)

Schools outside of the Free Education/Block Grant Scheme with an enrolment of 500 students or more receive an allocation of 1 post, while such schools with an enrolment of between 350 and 499 receive an allocation of 0.5 of a post.

In May 2005 additional funding for guidance was announced and the Department of Education and Science revised the allocation of hours for the provision of guidance in schools in the Free Education Scheme, while the allocation for schools outside the Free Education Scheme remained unchanged. The new system of allocation involves greater levels of guidance hours and a more finely graduated guidance allocation across school sizes. There is no differentiation across designated disadvantaged and non-designated disadvantaged schools.

Additional resources are allocated to designated schools under different disadvantaged areas schemes implemented in 1988/89, 1990/91, 1991/92 and 1994/95. Under these schemes, designated schools are allocated an additional ex-quota post. A small number of schools are allocated more than one such post. Some schools use such additional resources for guidance provision.

Community and comprehensive schools and community colleges are also allocated an ex-quota Chaplain post which is filled on the nomination of the relevant religious authority.

Table 1.2: Allocation of guidance hours, 2005/06 academic year

Recognised Pupil Enrolment	Allocation
1,000+	2.2 posts (47 hrs/wk)
900–999	1.7 posts (38 hrs/wk)
800–899	1.6 posts (36 hrs/wk)
700–799	1.4 posts (30 hrs/wk)
600–699	1.3 posts (28 hrs/wk)
500–599	1.1 post (24 hrs/wk)
400–499	0.8 post (17 hrs/wk)
300–399	0.6 post (13 hrs/wk)
200–299	0.5 post (11 hrs/wk)
<200	0.4 post (8 hrs/wk)

Guidance Enhancement Initiative

Additional guidance allocations are made to schools which were selected under the Guidance Enhancement Initiative (GEI). A total of 50 whole-time equivalent posts were allocated to 103 schools under this Initiative with effect from 2001/02 on the basis of an expert evaluation of schools' applications. The GEI was extended for a further two years and an additional 30 guidance posts (78 schools) were created on a temporary basis under this Initiative from the commencement of the 2004/05 school year.

All schools were invited to apply by submitting detailed proposals on how they would use the additional hours to enhance their current guidance programmes. The aim (of both phases of the initiative) is to support schools in developing innovative ways of enhancing guidance under three strands (Department of Education and Science, press release, 12 July 2004):

- Assisting schools to combat early school leaving;
- Promoting the uptake of science subjects in senior cycle; and
- Developing links between schools, business, voluntary, state and local agencies.

1.4 INTERNATIONAL CONTEXT

International work (OECD, CEDEFOP and World Bank reports) has tended to focus attention on the nature of career guidance services operating in schools, giving considerably less attention to the more "personal counselling" dimension of the role which has traditionally been a feature of Guidance Counselling services in Irish schools. In terms of such career guidance, Watts and Sultana (2003) noted a great deal of inter-country convergence in the practice of career guidance. However, they did observe some specific differences between countries, including differences between educational systems with strong early-streaming and tracking mechanisms and those with more flexible pathways: guidance services tend to play a more important role in the latter than in the former. They also note differences between countries in which most public services – including career guidance services – are delivered by the state or state agencies, and countries in which there has been a strong policy to deliver services through the private and voluntary sectors wherever possible: the latter tends to lead to a greater diversity of service provision.

Many countries, like Ireland, have Guidance Counsellors with a more holistic role covering personal and social as well as educational and vocational guidance as shown in Table 1.3. Austria, Denmark, Germany, Spain and Sweden all have specialist teachers within schools to deliver guidance services similar to the position of "Guidance Counsellors" in Ireland.[2] Austria, France, Germany, Luxembourg and Spain also have outside specialists similar to the National Educational Psychological Service (NEPS). Guidance in most European countries covers a combination of vocational, personal and educational guidance and Germany, Luxembourg and Spain also incorporate an element of learning and/or behavioural support. Germany and Spain are the only two countries that explicitly state that they offer personal guidance to their students in a similar fashion to Ireland (www.Eurydice.org). Germany, for example, appears to have a similar system to Ireland with "counselling teachers" who are "members of staff with extra training in educational science and psychology".

---

[2] While some of these countries are early trackers where career guidance services play an important role, they also adopt a holistic model incorporating personal and social guidance within the Guidance Counsellor's role.

Table 1.3: Summary of guidance in European countries from Eurydice information

Country	Who Delivers Guidance?			What Does Guidance Cover?			
	All Teachers	Specialist Teachers	Outside Specialists	Vocational Guidance	Personal Guidance	Educational Guidance	Learning and/or Behavioural Support
Austria	✓	✓	✓	✓		✓	
Denmark	✓	✓		✓		✓	
France			✓	✓		✓	
Germany		✓	✓	✓	✓	✓	✓
Ireland		✓	✓	✓	✓	✓	
Italy				✓		✓	
Luxembourg				✓		✓	✓
Spain	✓	✓	✓	✓	✓	✓	✓
Sweden		✓		✓		✓	

School psychological services "offer individual assistance using psychological diagnosis, counselling and treatment methods". In Spain, the first support for students is the form teacher or tutor. Supplementing this is a Guidance Department within each school. Schools in Spain also have specialist "sector counselling teams". These teams incorporate educational psychologists, social workers, speech therapists and learning support teachers. The counselling departments within the schools provide the form teachers with support to provide counselling services.

However, within such "holistic" systems like Ireland, economic commentators warn that there is a danger that career and educational guidance in schools can be marginalised within the broad concept of guidance. They maintain that there are two ways this may happen: (1) the pressing nature of the personal and behavioural problems of a minority of pupils mean that Guidance Counsellors spend much of their time on these problems, at the expense of the help needed by all pupils in relation to their educational and vocational choices; and (2) guidance on such choices tends to focus mainly on educational choices as ends in themselves, rather than on their vocational implications and on longer-term career planning (Watts and Sultana, 2003). They point to two countries, Norway and Poland, which are separating out a distinct career guidance role, partly to protect its resourcing and partly to address its distinctive competence requirements, including knowledge of the labour market (for such a career role).

Countries also vary in the extent to which guidance is incorporated into the mainstream curriculum or treated as a separate, and perhaps more specialist, function. In the United States, for example, guidance is usually provided by specialist school counsellors similar to Guidance Counsellors in Ireland. The most common model of guidance in the United States is the "Missouri Comprehensive Guidance Program Model" which is practiced in most states in the US. The program has four key parts: Guidance Curriculum, Individual Planning, Responsive Services and System Support (Ellis, 1990). This model also incorporates guidance into the curriculum and appears to be quite unique in this respect. The guidance curriculum is delivered through classroom activities and is structured around career planning, knowledge of self and others and educational development. The model attempts to integrate guidance, through the curriculum, into all aspects of school life. Canada's curricular component guidance system is also based on the United States model.

Denmark also appears to include *some* provision for guidance in the curriculum. In many respects, Ireland incorporates guidance in a more limited way into the curriculum in that "Guidance informs part of the curriculum in senior cycle through the Transition Year, Leaving Certificate Applied and Leaving Certificate Vocational Programmes" (Eurydice, 2005). Apart from these specific programmes, guidance is not generally incorporated into the curriculum in Ireland.

A number of other countries make career guidance available in specialist form from the employment service or some other agency based outside the school, in addition to career education and guidance within the school itself. Germany and the UK operate such a system, and a number of countries are exploring the possibility of setting up agencies of this kind. They note the importance of a clear partnership between schools and these specialist agencies to avoid confusion and unnecessary overlap.

Clearly there is no one model of guidance service for second-level students: wide variations exist in terms of the organisation and structure of guidance services, the nature of delivery and the breadth of the "guidance" role. While Ireland is by no means unique in the nature of its guidance services, it is among a minority of countries offering a holistic role covering personal counselling in addition to educational and career guidance. There is a lack of information on the extent to which external support services play a role in providing personal and social support for students in Ireland. The present study will address this gap, as well as giving some attention to the role of the private sector in meeting guidance/counselling needs. In addition, the extent to which career guidance provision is structured within the curriculum is unclear, as is the professional identity and qualifications of Guidance Counsellors. These are some of the issues this study explores.

1.5 FOCUS OF THE STUDY

As noted, the importance of guidance counselling provision at second-level has been highlighted by a number of sources and major reviews by the OECD, CEDEFOP and the World Bank highlight the prominence of the issue in European and international contexts. This reflects the importance of guidance and counselling services in the current and lifelong educational, labour market and personal experiences of young people as they progress through life. Educational decisions (such as subject choice and senior cycle programme choice) have serious implications for the nature and breadth of educational and labour market options available to young people as they leave school and thereafter. The issue of gender and socio-economic segregation in occupational sectors is particularly pertinent. In addition, career guidance experiences at second level are likely to be related to educational success at further and third level education, as recent research (Healy, Carpenter and Lynch, 1999) illustrates an association between inadequate career guidance, unclear career aspirations and non-completion at third level.

Guidance also has a key role to play in ensuring educational retention and raising awareness of the potentially negative consequences of early school leaving. Indeed, there is an important need to ensure that *all* students receive adequate information on their choices both within school and post school. In addition, there is the issue of schools as "sites for intervention" or at least places where behavioural and social problems manifest themselves. In this respect, it seems that it is timely to look at the role and effectiveness of school guidance provision. Finally, career "skills", such as the ability to source and process career information, career planning, job search and career management, are also important components of effective guidance preparation.

However, there is a lack of understanding of the nature and impact of guidance services in Irish second-level schools and, crucially, the extent of variation in provision across schools. While the literature and research on guidance provision and the role of Guidance Counsellors in schools has grown over the years,[3] a lack of information remains about the delivery of guidance services within post-primary schools and the role of

---

[3] See, for example, publications by the National Centre for Guidance in Education: Guidelines for the Practice of Guidance and Counselling, 1996; Careers Information Materials in Irish Schools, 1997; Principals' Perceptions of the Guidance Service in Post-primary Schools, 1997; National Centre for Guidance in Education Review, 1999; Guidance and Counselling in Post-primary schools, pilot, 1999; and Planning the School Guidance Programme, 2004.

Guidance Counsellors. While the role of Guidance Counsellors has remained largely for schools to decide, there is a lack of understanding of
the implications of such "discretion" for services across schools and the
exact nature and comprehensiveness of the service being offered to students. To what extent, for example, do Guidance Counsellors offer a holistic role to their students encompassing personal/social support as well as
educational/career advice? Do Guidance Counsellors offer a service to all
students or is their role more narrowly confined to senior cycle students?
To what extent does this vary and what are the implications of such variations (if any) for students' decision-making and educational choices?

As noted earlier, studies have identified a need to examine students'
own satisfaction with their guidance experiences with a view to determining how students felt those experiences had helped them in making
personal, educational and career decisions.

This study addresses these and other aspects of guidance services in
second-level schools. The study comprehensively examines the experiences and views of providers and consumers of guidance services in
schools, namely the Principals, Guidance Counsellors and students themselves. It also considers the role and comprehensiveness of external support services for schools and the adequacy of training provision. The study
combines both qualitative and quantitative methodologies, utilising a mix-
ture of research methods: in-depth semi structured interviews and analysis
of self-completed questionnaires. Such a "mixed-method" approach
strengthens the study in a number of ways. First, national data from questionnaires provide an overall picture of guidance services at second-level
in Ireland. Second, in-depth interviews explore the voices of the key personnel in the case study schools and enable the researchers to tap rich information which would not have otherwise been possible.

The following research questions guide the study:

1. What is the nature of pastoral and general support structures for stu-
    dents in second-level schools? How do these support structures vary
    across schools? What is the level of satisfaction with support struc-
    tures for students?

2. What role do Guidance Counsellors play in second-level schools?
    How does their role fit into more general pastoral care arrange-

ments? How does their role vary across year groups and senior cycle programmes? How does their role vary across school types, size and schools serving socio-economically diverse groups?

3. What are the views of the key stakeholders (management, Guidance Counsellors and students) on the level of resources for guidance services?

4. How is guidance information presented to students and what are the methodologies employed?

5. Are students satisfied with existing guidance counselling services in their schools?

6. To what extent do guidance services in schools encompass a "whole school" approach and contact with external supports/agencies?

7. What impact has the Guidance Enhancement Initiative had on guidance services in schools and on the levels of satisfaction with guidance provision?

1.6 METHODOLOGY

As discussed, the study was undertaken in two phases. The first involved a quantitative postal survey targeting 260 schools across the country. Schools were selected to be nationally representative by school type and size. Questionnaires were administered to Principals, Guidance Counsellors and teachers with an allocation of guidance hours. The achieved sample was 168 Principals, giving a response rate of 65 per cent, and 188 Guidance Counsellors or teachers with guidance duties, giving at least one Guidance Counsellor in 57 per cent of the schools surveyed. The data were re-weighted to adjust for school sector, school size and disadvantaged status.

Data from this phase of the study were used to identify 15 schools for more in-depth case-study analysis. These schools were selected to represent a number of dimensions of guidance provision, as well as more structural features of schools. There were two main aspects of guidance provision which informed the selection:

1. Level of guidance provision: both the number of Guidance Counsellors and the hours allocated to guidance were considered.

2. Breadth of activities of Guidance Counsellor: the number of areas (such as career advice, assessment, subject choice/level advice, personal and social support) where the Guidance Counsellor felt they played an important role.

In addition, the selection ensured the inclusion of schools participating in the Guidance Enhancement Initiative (GEI, see below for further information on this Initiative): in total two of the 15 schools participate in the GEI, with different levels of GEI resources allocated to the two schools. Further details regarding the guidance resources of the 15 case study schools are presented in Chapter Four.

Schools were also selected to ensure a broad and representative mix of schools according to four main criteria:

1. School type and gender;

2. School size (closely related to level of Guidance Counselling provision);

3. Regional location; and

4. Designated disadvantaged status.

In-depth interviews with Principals, Deputy Principals, Guidance Counsellors and other personnel with a pastoral care role were undertaken within the schools. Interviews with key personnel were supplemented with group interviews with Junior and Leaving Certificate students within the schools. These interviews were recorded and transcribed. The transcripts were coded using the QSR N6 software package to identify the main themes emerging from the interviews. These case studies allow us to provide a detailed picture of the operation of guidance services on the ground within schools serving different groups of students. They crucially also present the perspective of the student: their views on the kinds of guidance and counselling services they have received and their observations on improvements that might be needed. Details of the case study schools are presented in Table 1.4; pseudonyms are used to identify schools.

Table 1.4: Summary of case study schools

School Name	Type	Size	Designated Disadvantaged	Guidance Allocation
Low Guidance Provision, Low Range of Activities				
1. Hills Road	Girls' secondary	Small–Medium	No	11 hours
2. Beechwood Square	Girls' secondary	Medium	No	11 hours
Low Guidance Provision, High Range of Activities				
3. Whitefield	Coed Secondary	Large	No	22 hours
4. Rosendale	Vocational	Medium	Yes	22 hours
5. Willow Grove	Community/comprehensive	Small	No	1.5 days/wk
Medium Guidance Provision, Medium Range of Activities				
6. *Laurel Park*	*Community/comprehensive*	*Medium*	*Yes*	*44 hours*
7. Oakhill Way	Private Coed Secondary	Medium	No	11 hours
8. Maplewood	Girls' Secondary	Medium–Large	No	32 hours
9. Lawton Way	Boys' Secondary	Small	Yes	22 hours

Table 1.4: Summary of case study schools (continued)

School Name	Type	Size	Designated Disadvantaged	Guidance Allocation
High Guidance Provision, High Range of Activities				
10. Ashfield Park	*Vocational*	*Medium*	*Yes*	*33 hours*
11. Seaview	Community/comprehensive	Medium–Large	Yes	22 hours
12. Chestnut Drive	Coed Secondary	Large	No	19 hours
High Guidance Provision, Low Range of Activities				
13. Riverbank	Boys' Secondary	Medium–Large	No	22 hours
14. Greenwood	Community/Comprehensive	Large	No	22 hours
15. Cherryfield View	Vocational	Medium	No	18 hours

Note: Italic type indicates GEI schools.

Finally, the analysis draws on the "Annual School Leavers' Survey of 2002". This survey provides an insight into the position, experiences and attitudes of schools leavers approximately one year after they have left second-level education. The survey is based on a stratified random sample of those leaving the official second-level system, with respondents being interviewed between 12 and 18 months after leaving school. The data provide a valuable insight into the nature of guidance and advice young people report receiving while at second-level school. It also allows an examination of the nature and extent of guidance according to educational attainment and gender, looking, for example, at the key sources, if any, of educational and career advice reported by early school leavers relative to those who completed their second-level education.

1.7 STRUCTURE OF THE BOOK

This study takes the following format. Chapter Two presents the views of School Principals from the national survey, exploring their attitudes on, and experiences of, the guidance services in their schools. A similar format is adopted in Chapter Three, drawing on the experiences and views of Guidance Counsellors themselves. Chapter Four turns attention to the case study material examining the detailed structure and nature of guidance and support services in the case study schools, from the perspectives of School Principals and Guidance Counsellors. Chapter Five directs attention to students' experiences of guidance and counselling; drawing first on national School Leavers' Survey data and second on their views from focus groups in the case study schools. Some key issues and tensions for schools in defining and presenting their guidance services are explored in Chapter Six. Chapter Seven explores the extent of variation across schools in the nature of guidance provision. In addition, the chapter considers the views of key personnel in terms of some of the key strengths, weaknesses and priorities for the future of guidance. Finally, Chapter Eight considers some of the main findings and discusses the implications for policy and practice at school and departmental levels.

Chapter Two

PRINCIPALS' VIEWS OF GUIDANCE SERVICES

2.1 INTRODUCTION

Drawing on the postal survey of 168 school Principals, this chapter examines Principals' views on, and attitudes to, guidance services in their schools. The chapter begins with a review of overall support structures in schools. The nature of general support structures or pastoral care systems is considered, along with the extent to which Principals are satisfied with current provision. Section 2.3 examines the involvement of Guidance Counsellors across the areas of academic, vocational and personal/social guidance. Finally, Section 2.4 explores the attitudes and views of Principals regarding guidance services in their school, the level of resources for guidance, the adequacy of the service and the perceived views of other staff in the school. A similar format is adopted in Chapter Three, drawing on the experiences of Guidance Counsellors themselves.

2.2 GENERAL SUPPORT STRUCTURES

2.2.1 Pastoral care programmes

The vast majority of second-level schools (84 per cent) have a pastoral care programme in place for their students. Such programmes generally apply to all students in the school, although in some cases a more targeted approach is taken; 76 per cent of the programmes apply to all students, 16 per cent to junior cycle students only, 4 per cent to senior cycle students only and 2 per cent to first years only.

In just over half of cases where there was a pastoral care or other personal/social development programme in place for students, this programme was based on a Class Tutor system. Another very prevalent approach was a Year Head system, which operated in 42 per cent of schools. Social, Personal and Health Education (SPHE) was mentioned in a further 31 per cent of cases and a pastoral care team was also mentioned in 21 per cent of cases. Guidance was specifically mentioned in only 9 per cent of cases.[4]

2.2.2 Specific support structures

In addition to asking Principals about general support structures in the school, the survey captured important information on the extent to which schools had put specific support structures in place for certain groups of students: these included those with learning difficulties, those from the non-national community and those from the Travelling community. The vast majority of schools (91 per cent) have supports in place for students with learning difficulties. These supports typically centre on learning support teachers, resource and special needs teachers and small group tuition. Amongst Principals surveyed, 79 per cent also said they have specific supports for students with special needs (disabilities). These provisions centred on learning supports, resource/special needs teachers and Special Needs Assistants (SNAs). In total, 44 per cent of Principals reported that their school had specific support structures in place for non-national students. These supports were mainly related to extra English classes or TEFL teachers along with providing access to learning support and resource teachers. A majority (62 per cent) of Principals stated that they did not have any specific supports in place for students from Travelling families. Those who reported providing supports mainly provided extra learning support.

Schools varied in the extent to which they had supports in place for the specified groups of students. Of Principals surveyed, 40 per cent reported having two of the above support structures, over a quarter had

---

[4] Percentages add to more than 100 as more than one item could be mentioned.

three such supports in place with a fifth having support structures for all specified categories of students (see Figure 2.1).

Figure 2.1: The number of specific support structures

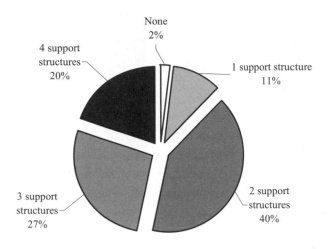

2.2.3 Satisfaction with support structures

Generally, second-level school Principals were satisfied or very satisfied (61 per cent) with the overall support structures in place in their school (see Figure 2.2). However, a sizeable minority of the schools were either dissatisfied or very dissatisfied (22 per cent) with support structures in the school. While the majority of Principals across all school types express satisfaction, some variation by school type is evident, although the difference is not statistically significant. In particular, Principals in girls' secondary schools were on average more satisfied (69 per cent) with the support structures in their school while vocational school Principals were least likely to state that they were very satisfied or satisfied with support structures in their school (56 per cent).

Figure 2.2: Satisfaction with support structures and school type

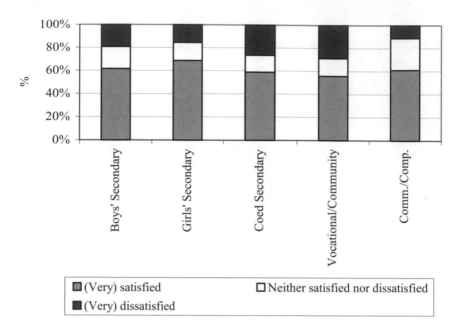

Smaller schools on average reported somewhat higher dissatisfaction levels, although differences by school size were not marked. Disadvantaged status schools were significantly more likely than non-disadvantaged schools to report that they were satisfied or very satisfied with the support structures in their school (71 per cent as compared to 57 per cent of non-disadvantaged schools, see Figure 2.3). However, there were no significant differences in levels of satisfaction reported among Principals according to the reported rates of literacy and numeracy problems in the school.

As might be expected, those Principals in schools with a pastoral care programme in place are somewhat more likely to be satisfied or very satisfied with the support structures in their school, although the differences are not statistically significant (see Figure 2.4).

Figure 2.3: Satisfaction with support structures by disadvantaged status

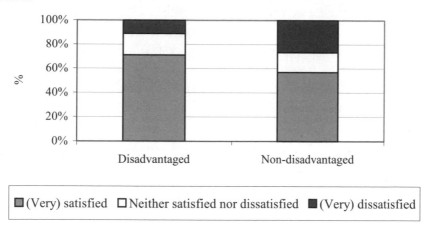

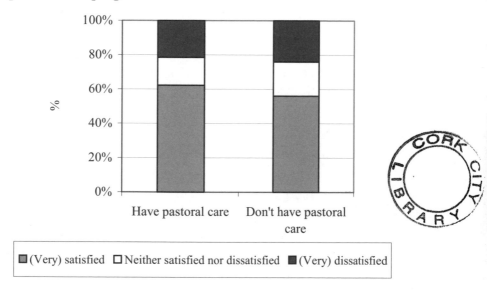

Figure 2.4: Satisfaction with supports for students and whether school has pastoral care programme

Interestingly, there was a significant difference in overall satisfaction levels between those schools where the Principal reported a higher frequency of involvement of the Guidance Counsellor in activities in the

school, such as assisting students with learning difficulties and so-
cial/personal support, and those who had a lower frequency of reported
Guidance Counsellor involvement. Principals in schools where Guidance
Counsellors were more involved in the school were significantly more
satisfied with the support structures in their school (see Figure 2.5).

***Figure 2.5: Satisfaction with support structures and Guidance
Counsellor's involvement in activities***

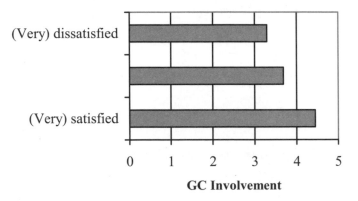

Schools that were taking part in the Guidance Enhancement Initiative
(GEI) were on average more satisfied with the overall support systems
for students in their school, indicating that satisfaction is, at least partly,
related to the resources available for guidance as well as the involvement
of the Guidance Counsellor in the school. However, this difference was
not statistically significant.

When Principals were asked what other supports they would like to
see in place for students, over a quarter (29 per cent) responded that they
would like to see more guidance hours or an improved ratio of Guidance
Counsellors to students. A further quarter said they would like counselling, including bereavement counselling, to be available.

2.2.4 Liaison with external services/agencies

As well as having support structures in place within the school, many
schools had links with external services and agencies in relation to student welfare. The vast majority (almost 90 per cent) of Principals reported that their school liaised with the National Educational Psycho-

logical Service (NEPS) to a great or some extent. Two-thirds said that they liaised with Social Workers, while just under half had contact with the National Education Welfare Board (School Attendance Officer). Just under half had liaised with Juvenile Liaison Officers or the Gardai, 36 per cent with Youthreach and almost one-third with Youth Workers (see Figure 2.6).

Figure 2.6: Per cent of schools that liaise with external services/agencies

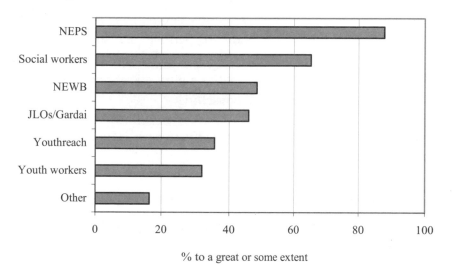

% to a great or some extent

2.3 NATURE OF GUIDANCE ACTIVITIES AND INVOLVEMENT

Chapter One discussed the holistic role adopted by Guidance Counsellors in Ireland compared to the position in many other Western countries. However, comparatively little is known about the relative involvement of Guidance Counsellors in different areas within second-level schools. This section discusses the involvement of Guidance Counsellors in 'core' activities and in a broader range of areas within the school. Their involvement in guiding students on subject choice and in the management structures of the school is also examined.

2.3.1 Guidance Counsellor's involvement in main activities

Figure 2.7 illustrates the role of Guidance Counsellors across a range of academic, vocational and personal areas from the perspective of school Principals. Almost all Principals (99 per cent) reported that the Guidance Counsellor(s) in their school was either to a great extent or to some extent involved in vocational or career-related support and guidance. Similarly, the vast majority (94 per cent) stated that the Guidance Counsellor was involved in general academic support and guidance to a great extent or to some extent. This would include guidance on subject choice as well as on the selection of subject levels for exam purposes. The next most important activity related to the area of personal and social support or counselling: 84 per cent of Principals reported that the Guidance Counsellors in their schools were involved to a great extent or to some extent with social/personal support and counselling.

Figure 2.7: Guidance Counsellor's involvement in main activities (great/some extent)

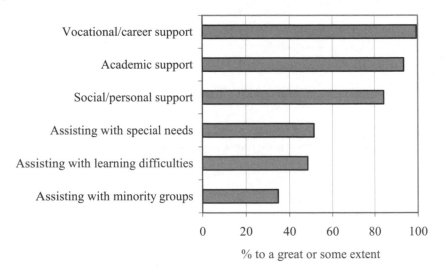

Guidance Counsellors were not as involved when it came to assisting students with special needs, students with learning difficulties or students from minority groups. Nearly two-thirds (62 per cent) of Principals reported that their Guidance Counsellor was not to any extent or not to any great extent involved in assisting students from minority groups with 4 per cent explicitly stating that there were no such students in the school. Over half (51 per cent) of Principals reported that the Guidance Counsellor in their school was to a great extent or to some extent involved in assisting students with special needs. A similar proportion (49 per cent) reported that the Guidance Counsellor was involved to a great or some extent with assisting students with learning difficulties.

There is some variation in Guidance Counsellor involvement in various activities across different types of school. Having increased resources for guidance appears to facilitate greater involvement in general academic support, personal support and assisting students with special needs. In very small schools (<250 students), Guidance Counsellors are much less likely to be involved in general academic support than in larger schools. Guidance Counsellors in GEI schools are more likely to be involved in personal support/counselling and in assisting students with special needs than in non-GEI schools. In designated disadvantaged schools, Guidance Counsellors are also more likely to be involved in assisting students with special needs, perhaps reflecting different needs among the student cohort. In general, having more guidance personnel allows schools to expand provision beyond a focus on career guidance; schools with two or more staff involved in guidance tend to have greater Guidance Counsellor involvement across a range of activities. As might be expected, there was a significant relationship between the number of specific support structures in place and the extent to which the Guidance Counsellor was reported to be involved in a wide range of activities.

2.3.2 Guidance Counsellor involvement in broader activities

The survey data also captured the involvement of Guidance Counsellors in a wider range of activities, including ability-testing, student work experience and contact with parents, for example (see Figure 2.8). Providing career/employment-related guidance and academic guidance continued to be the two most important Guidance Counsellor activities with almost all (96-97 per cent) Principals indicating that these activities are an important or very important part of the Guidance Counsellor's role in their school. Providing personal and social guidance was also reported to be very important or important by 90 per cent of Principals. Guidance Counsellors were also reported by the majority of Principals to be very important or important in dealing with ability testing (88 per cent).

Figure 2.8: Importance of Guidance Counsellors in specified activities

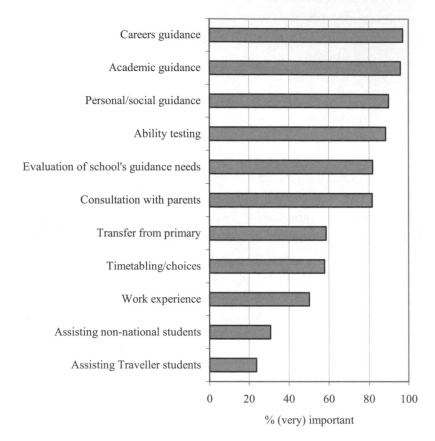

% (very) important

Four-fifths (82 per cent) of Principals reported that the Guidance Counsellor played an important role in the evaluation of the school's guidance needs. A similar proportion of Principals consider consultation with parents to be a key activity of the Guidance Counsellor.

Activities in which Guidance Counsellors were not considered to be as involved were assisting with the transfer from primary to secondary school (59 per cent), organising subject choices/packages/timetabling (58 per cent) and dealing with work experience (50 per cent). Assisting non-national students and assisting students from traveller families was not seen as a very important part of the Guidance Counsellor's role. Only 31 per cent of Principals indicated that assisting non-nationals was an important or very important activity of the Guidance Counsellor, and just under a quarter indicated that assisting students from Traveller families was important.

When the Principals were asked what they considered to be the single most important activity of the Guidance Counsellor in the school, providing personal and social guidance was mentioned in 37 per cent of cases, providing careers-related advice was mentioned in 34 per cent of cases, while providing academic guidance (12 per cent) was the next most important activity listed by Principals.

2.3.3 Approaches to subject choice at junior cycle and the role of the Guidance Counsellor

There are three main approaches to subject choice at junior cycle taken by second-level schools. In total, 29 per cent of schools allow students to try out subjects for the whole of first year before they choose their Junior Certificate subjects. In 29 per cent of schools, students choose their subjects before entering first year and a further 25 per cent of schools let students try out subjects for part of first year before choosing (see Table 2.1).

Table 2.1: Approach to subject choice at junior cycle

Choice	%
Students do not have a choice of subjects	9.8
Students choose before entering 1st year	28.5
Students try out subjects for part of 1st year	25.2
Students try out subjects for whole of 1st year	29.2
Other	7.3
Total N	164

At junior cycle stage, the main person mentioned by school Principals with responsibility for advising students on subject choice in the school is the Guidance Counsellor (mentioned in 71 per cent of cases). School

Principals were mentioned in almost half of the cases, subject teachers in 41 per cent of schools and Year Heads and Deputy Principals were both mentioned 22-23 per cent of the time.

The role of the Guidance Counsellor in subject choice decisions at junior cycle clearly depends on the timing of subject choice. In schools where Principals reported that the students choose their subjects before entering first year, the person with greatest responsibility for advising students on subject choice at junior cycle was the school Principal (mentioned in 67 per cent of cases). However, Guidance Counsellors continued to play an important role in subject choice in these schools and were mentioned in 63 per cent of cases.[5]

In schools where the Principal reported that students try out subjects for part of first year before choosing, the Guidance Counsellor played a stronger role and was mentioned in 71 per cent of such schools. Subject teachers also play an important role in these schools and were mentioned in 52 per cent of cases. In schools where the Principal reported that students try out subjects for all of first year, a similar pattern was observed. Guidance Counsellors were mentioned in 81 per cent of cases and subject teachers were mentioned in 53 per cent of cases. It appears that the role of the Principal in advising students on subject choice in the junior cycle diminishes when students are allowed to choose their subjects after they start in the school and have an opportunity to try out subjects for a period of time.

At senior cycle stage, the key role of Guidance Counsellors in advising students on their choice of subjects is apparent. Guidance Counsellors were mentioned in 94 per cent of cases, subject teachers in 46 per cent of cases, school Principals in 41 per cent of cases and both Deputy Principals and Year Heads were mentioned in 23 per cent of cases.

2.3.4 Interaction of Principals and Guidance Counsellors

Questions were included in the survey to identify the frequency with which the Principal and Guidance Counsellor meet. The greatest proportion (39 per cent) of school Principals reported that they formally meet with their Guidance Counsellor(s) in relation to guidance issues when a

---

[5] Percentages add to more than 100 as Principals could pick more than one option.

specific issue emerges. Almost a third (30 per cent) meet with the Guidance Counsellor(s) once a week with 13 per cent meeting formally every day (see Table 2.2).

Table 2.2: Frequency of meetings between Principal and Guidance Counsellor

	%
Every day	12.9
Once a week	30.2
Once a month	12.7
Less than once a month	5.3
When a specific issue emerges	38.9
Total N	166

2.3.5 Written guidance plan

The majority (71 per cent) of schools report having no written guidance plan in place. Of those Principals who reported that they have a written guidance plan, it is mainly Guidance Counsellors and Principals who have been involved in drawing up the plan. Guidance Counsellors were mentioned in 94 per cent of cases and Principals in 76 per cent of cases.

Interestingly, there is no clear-cut relationship between guidance resources and having a written guidance plan. There was no difference between those schools where there was a written guidance plan and schools who did not in terms of the number of teachers they had with specific guidance hours. As one might expect, those who report having a guidance plan tend to be somewhat more satisfied with the support structures in their school than those Principals who report not having a guidance plan. Almost a quarter of those with a written guidance plan are very satisfied compared to 14 per cent of those with no written plan.

2.4 SATISFACTION WITH GUIDANCE PROVISION

Generally school Principals were satisfied or very satisfied with the guidance services their school provided. A total of 86 per cent were (very) satisfied with vocational/career guidance in the school and similarly 85 per cent were (very) satisfied with academic guidance in the school. Principals were somewhat less satisfied with personal/social Guidance and counselling (67 per cent) or with the input into pastoral care provision (65 per cent). This indicates a gap between careers/ academic guidance provision and social/personal guidance provision.

In general, satisfaction levels were similar across the school sectors, different sizes of school and schools with varying levels of literacy and numeracy problems. Schools that were taking part in the Guidance Enhancement Initiative (GEI) were on average more satisfied with personal/social guidance and counselling and the input into Pastoral Care for students in their school, as were designated disadvantaged schools. However, such variation was not marked. Satisfaction with guidance provision was clearly related to the level of involvement of Guidance Counsellors in a wide range of activities in the school: the more involved Guidance Counsellors were, the more Principals reported being satisfied. Thus, there was a significant relationship between the level of involvement of the Guidance Counsellor in activities in the school such as assisting students with learning difficulties and social/personal support and how satisfied Principals were with guidance services.

2.4.1 Principals' opinions on the attitudes and capabilities of students in the school

Arising from differences in student intake, schools may vary in the extent to which students are oriented to higher education rather than direct entry into employment. The vast majority (88 per cent) of Principals either strongly agreed or agreed with the statement "students have a good idea how to apply for college". Similarly, 83 per cent agreed or strongly agreed with the statement that "students have a good idea how to apply for jobs". The majority of Principals (65 per cent) disagree or strongly disagree with the statement "students have low aspirations when it comes to thinking about college".

Principals in voluntary secondary schools were significantly more likely to agree or strongly agree with the statement that their students had a good idea how to apply for college compared to those in vocational schools and community/comprehensive schools (See Table 2.3). However, somewhat surprisingly, the pattern of responses did not vary significantly between designated disadvantaged and non-disadvantaged schools.

Table 2.3: "Students have a good idea how to apply for college"

	Secondary (%)	Vocational (%)	Community/ comprehensive (%)
Agree strongly/agree	94.7	79.6	80.0
Neither agree nor disagree	0.0	11.1	10.0
Disagree strongly/disagree	5.3	9.3	10.0
Total N	88	56	23

There were no significant differences between types of schools (in terms of sector or disadvantaged status) in whether the Principals reported that they thought students had a good idea of how to apply for jobs. However, there was a significant difference between school types in the extent to which Principals reported that they thought students had low aspirations for the future (See Table 2.4); students in vocational schools were seen as having significantly lower aspirations than their counterparts in voluntary secondary schools. Principals of smaller schools (<400 students) were more likely to agree that their students had low aspirations for the future, a pattern that holds within school sectors. Designated disadvantaged schools were significantly more likely to strongly agree or agree with the statement that students have low aspirations when it comes to thinking about their future (see Figure 2.9).

Table 2.4: "Students have low aspirations for the future"

	Secondary (%)	Vocational (%)	Community/ comprehensive (%)
Agree strongly/agree	16.0	27.8	21.1
Neither agree nor disagree	8.5	24.1	15.8
Disagree strongly/disagree	75.5	48.1	63.2
Total N	88	56	23

Figure 2.9: "Low aspirations for the future" and designated disadvantaged status

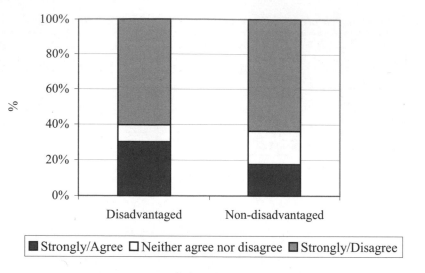

2.4.2 Principals' views regarding resources, guidance services and staff views

Principals were asked the extent to which they agreed with a number of statements relating to the resources available for guidance, the guidance services and the views of staff concerning guidance. In keeping with the patterns discussed above, the majority of Principals felt that their school had a well-developed pastoral care system and that students could generally avail of guidance services when necessary. In the majority of cases, the Guidance Counsellor was seen as having a strong involvement in the formulation of guidance policy. However, more negatively, resource issues came to the fore with only a minority (40 per cent) of schools considering there were sufficient resources for the Guidance Counsellor's work.

The perceived inadequacy of resources was reflected in the two-thirds of Principals who agreed that some students were missing out on the guidance and counselling that they need. This pattern was evident across different kinds of schools. However, Principals of vocational schools were somewhat more likely than those in secondary or community/comprehensive schools to feel that students are missing out on guidance (71 per cent compared with 62 per cent and 65 per cent respectively), reflecting the smaller average size and therefore smaller guidance allocation among schools in this sector.

Another issue emerging is the extent to which guidance is seen as a whole school undertaking. The issue of subject choice is seen as a whole school issue with most Principals reporting the involvement of subject teachers in giving guidance and advice to students (Figure 2.10). In addition, most Principals felt that staff were able to identify "at risk" students for referral to the Guidance Counsellor, although it is a matter of concern that 40 per cent of Principals did not feel this to be the case. Guidance was not generally seen as taking time away from subject teaching although almost a third of school Principals agreed that there is insufficient appreciation of guidance and counselling among the staff in their school (see Figure 2.10). The extent to which guidance appeared to be a "whole school" endeavour does not vary systematically by school characteristics, such as sector, size and disadvantaged status, indicating the potential role of school-level policy and general school climate in creating such an integrated approach. The extent to which guidance is integrated into school activities is discussed in greater detail in relation to the case-study schools.

2.4.3 Suggestions in relation to guidance provision

The most important provision Principals wanted to see in place in their school was that there would be more guidance hours or an improved guidance ratio. This issue was mentioned in 63 per cent of cases. The need for (greater) counselling provision was also mentioned in 13 per cent of cases.

Reflecting on more general national guidance services, the most important provision that Principals would like to see is the same provision they wanted to see in their schools, more guidance hours or an improved guidance ratio (mentioned in 39 per cent of cases). Counselling was again mentioned in 12 per cent of cases. Other provisions mentioned included support from external agencies (8 per cent), more resources (8 per cent), in-service training (6 per cent), and having a guidance plan (3 per cent).

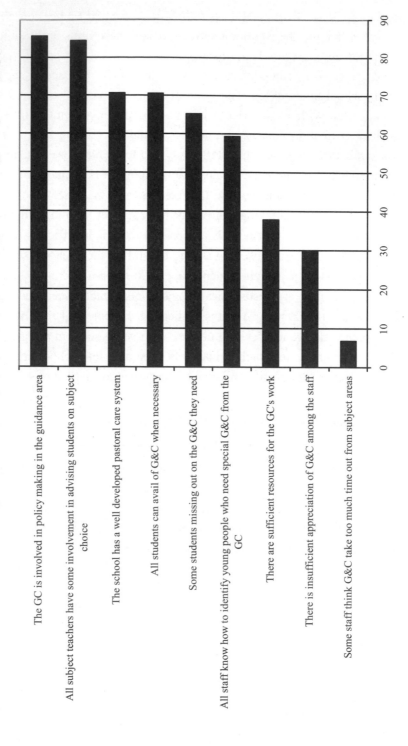

Figure 2.10: Views of principals regarding resources, guidance services and staff views (% agree/agree strongly)

2.5 SUMMARY AND DISCUSSION

The vast majority of schools have a pastoral care system in place for students and overall satisfaction levels with general support structures in schools are reasonable, although a considerable minority of schools are dissatisfied. Such general support structures also involve considerable contact with outside support services such as the National Educational Psychological Service, social workers and the National Educational Welfare Board. Satisfaction levels with support structures show some connection with guidance services: schools where Guidance Counsellors are involved in a wide range of activities report higher satisfaction levels.

In terms of the role of Guidance Counsellors, variation between schools is apparent. Involvement in vocational and career-related support and guidance is, according to Principals, almost universal, with strong involvement in academic support also apparent. The involvement of Guidance Counsellors in one aspect of academic guidance, advice on subject selection, however, depended on the timing of subject choice in the school. The third most important activity of the Guidance Counsellor was seen as relating to personal and social support/counselling. Satisfaction levels with the different activities tended to mirror the actual level of involvement, with relatively lower levels of satisfaction with personal/ social counselling. Interestingly, schools participating in the GEI had higher satisfaction with provision in the personal/social counselling area.

In spite of relatively high satisfaction levels with the three central aspects of guidance (career, academic and personal/social), many school Principals were dissatisfied with the resources available for guidance and a significant minority felt that students were missing out on the guidance and counselling that they need. Schools also varied in the extent to which guidance was integrated into the formal and informal structures of the school. Only a minority of school Principals held regular formal meetings with Guidance Counsellor(s) and relatively few schools had a written guidance plan in place. Furthermore, a significant minority of Principals reported a lack of appreciation of guidance counselling among the rest of the school staff.

Chapter Three

GUIDANCE COUNSELLORS' VIEWS OF GUIDANCE SERVICES

3.1 INTRODUCTION

Drawing on the postal survey of 188 Guidance Counsellors,[6] this chapter examines their views and attitudes across a range of areas concerned with guidance and counselling provision within second-level schools. Responses were received from an estimated 52 per cent of the total number of teachers involved in guidance in the 260 sampled schools and from at least one Guidance Counsellor in 57 per cent of the schools surveyed. The chapter begins with an overview of general support and pastoral care structures for students, along with the extent to which Guidance Counsellors are satisfied with current support structures. Section 3.3 examines actual levels of guidance provision across schools along with the levels of teaching demands being placed on Guidance Counsellors. The role of Guidance Counsellors is the subject of Section 3.4. This includes an examination of the involvement of Guidance Counsellors across the areas of academic, vocational and personal/social guidance. Finally, Section 3.5 explores the attitudes and views of Guidance Counsellors regarding the guidance services in their school, the level of resources for guidance, the adequacy of the service and the perceived views of other staff in the school. A summary and discussion complete the chapter in Section 3.6.

---

[6] Throughout this book, the term "Guidance Counsellor" is used to refer to all staff who are allocated guidance hours.

3.2 GENERAL SUPPORT STRUCTURES

3.2.1 Pastoral care programmes in the schools

In keeping with the accounts of school Principals presented in Chapter Two, the vast majority (83 per cent) of Guidance Counsellors surveyed reported a pastoral care programme in place for students in their school. The three main approaches taken to pastoral care were Social, Personal and Health Education (SPHE) (mentioned by 42 per cent), a Class Tutor system (33 per cent) and a Year Head system (28 per cent). Interestingly, Guidance Counsellors were more likely to emphasise SPHE, and less likely to emphasise Class Tutors and Year Heads, as the basis for support arrangements than school Principals (see Chapter Two). When asked which staff members were involved in running the programme, Guidance Counsellors were the staff members most likely to be mentioned (29 per cent). Year Heads and Class Tutors were also mentioned frequently (28 per cent). Other staff mentioned included religion teachers (18 per cent), Chaplains (17 per cent), subject teachers (15 per cent) and SPHE teachers (13 per cent).

3.2.2 Satisfaction with support structures

Generally Guidance Counsellors were satisfied or very satisfied (63 per cent) with the support structures (see Figure 3.1), a similar level of satisfaction to that of school Principals (see Chapter Two). However, a significant minority of the Guidance Counsellors were either dissatisfied or very dissatisfied (22 per cent) with the support structures in their school.

There was significant variation across Guidance Counsellors in satisfaction levels with support structures, a pattern that was related to the school sector they worked in. Four-fifths of Guidance Counsellors in community/comprehensive schools were satisfied with the support system for students in their school and satisfaction levels were also relatively high in girls' secondary schools (see Figure 3.1). In contrast, just over half of those in vocational schools expressed satisfaction while Guidance Counsellors in boys' secondary schools were least likely to state that they were satisfied with support structures in the school (28 per cent). Guidance Counsellors in fee-paying secondary schools were also on average more satisfied than those in non-fee paying secondary schools (82 per cent compared to 60 per cent).

Figure 3.1: Proportion of Guidance Counsellors (very) satisfied with support structures

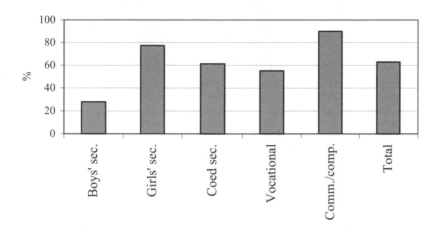

There were no significant differences in satisfaction levels according to school size, although Guidance Counsellors in larger schools are some-what more satisfied with student support structures then those in smaller schools. Similarly, there were no significant differences in satisfaction levels in schools according to designated disadvantaged status.

Guidance Counsellors in schools that were taking part in the Guidance Enhancement Initiative (GEI) were significantly more satisfied with the support systems for students in their school (see Figure 3.2). Almost four-fifths (88 per cent) of those taking part in the GEI were satisfied with the support systems compared to 59 per cent of those not in the GEI.

As might be expected, Guidance Counsellors in schools that have a pastoral care programme are significantly more likely to be satisfied or very satisfied with the support structures for students in their school. The majority (69 per cent) of Guidance Counsellors in schools with a pastoral care programme are (very) satisfied compared to only a third of those in schools without a pastoral care programme.

Figure 3.2: Proportion of Guidance Counsellors (very) satisfied with support structures by participation in GEI

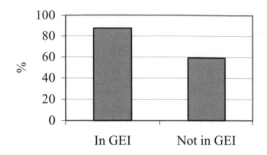

3.2.3 Liaison with external services/agencies

In addition to support structures within the school, Guidance Counsellors reported a good deal of contact between their school and external support services. In total, 89 per cent of Guidance Counsellors reported that their school liaised with the National Educational Psychological Service (NEPS) to a great or some extent. Three-quarters indicated that they liaised with Social Workers, while over half had liaised with the National Educational Welfare Board (School Attendance Officers). Over half (55 per cent) liaised with Juvenile Liaison Officers or the Gardaí, almost half with Youthreach and 35 per cent with Youth Workers.

The degree of contact between the school and external support services tended to reflect the nature of the student cohort with more extensive linkages evident among designated disadvantaged schools and less use of external support services among fee-paying secondary schools. Designated disadvantaged schools were significantly more likely to liaise with NEPS, the National Educational Welfare Board, Social Workers, Youthreach, Youth-workers and Juvenile Liaison Officers/Gardaí than non-disadvantaged status schools. A similar pattern was evident among schools taking part in the GEI with greater contact with the National Educational Welfare Board, Youthreach, Youth workers, Juvenile Liaison Officers/Gardaí and, to a lesser extent, Social Workers. This pattern is, however, likely to reflect the social profile of GEI schools rather than participation in the Initiative *per se*. In contrast, fee-paying schools were significantly less likely to liaise to any great extent with the National Educational Psychological Service, the National Educational Welfare Board, Social Workers, Youthreach and Juvenile Liaison Officers/Gardaí.

Contact with external agencies also appeared to be influenced by the level of resources and specialist personnel across schools. Very small schools (<250 students) were significantly less likely than other schools to liaise with NEPS and Social Workers. Larger schools (>600 students) are more likely to liaise with the Gardaí than other schools. Vocational schools, which were on average smaller than other schools, were significantly less likely to liaise to any great extent with NEPS and somewhat less likely to liaise with the National Educational Welfare Board compared to other types of schools.

3.3 GUIDANCE PROVISION

A total of 188 Guidance Counsellors returned questionnaires. Two-thirds of Guidance Counsellors in the survey were female. Just under half of the Guidance Counsellors surveyed were full-time Guidance Counsellors, 22 per cent were part-time Guidance Counsellors while 31 per cent were teachers with guidance hours. Because of differences in average school size, the secondary and vocational sectors are more reliant on part-time Guidance Counsellors and teachers with guidance hours than the community/comprehensive sector; 84 per cent of those in community/comprehensive schools describe themselves as full-time Guidance Counsellors compared with 50 per cent in secondary schools and 34 per cent in vocational schools. In terms of tenure, 81 per cent had a permanent whole-time appointment in the school, 2 per cent had a temporary whole-time post, 9 per cent were eligible part-time teachers and a further 7 per cent were part-time. Those in the secondary sector are somewhat more likely to be employed on a part-time basis than those in the other school types. Female Guidance Counsellors were more likely to be employed on a part-time basis than their male counterparts.

In total, 82 per cent described themselves as qualified Guidance Counsellors. There were significant differences between types of schools in whether the Guidance Counsellor was qualified or not. All Guidance Counsellors in community/comprehensive schools were qualified compared with around three-quarters of those in coeducational secondary and vocational schools. Qualification levels also varied by school size with smaller schools having a higher proportion of guidance staff without formal qualifications. The over-representation of unqualified Guidance Counsellors in smaller schools and schools in the vocational sector is due to the greater reliance of these schools on part-time guidance staff who are less likely to have formal guidance qualifications. Of guidance staff who were not qualified, under a quarter were undertaking a guidance/counselling-related course at the time of the survey.

Regarding their path to their current position, over half of the Guidance Counsellors surveyed indicated that they had not taught in that school before becoming the Guidance Counsellor. In terms of timing of their appointment, 63 per cent of the Guidance Counsellors surveyed were appointed to the position in their current school between 1993 and 2004. Almost a quarter were appointed between 1972 and 1982, and a further 15 per cent were appointed between 1983 and 1992. Almost a third of Guidance Counsellors surveyed have worked in the school for between 2 and 10 years, 21 per cent between 11 and 18 years, a quarter between 19 and 26 years and a quarter between 27 and 37 years.

Figure 3.3: Number of hours teaching among Guidance Counsellors with teaching commitments

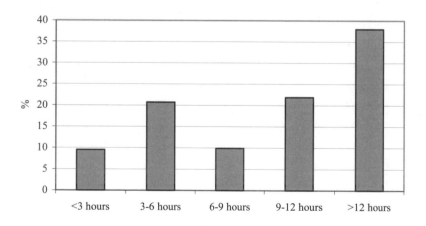

Over three-quarters of those surveyed had teaching commitments. Subjects most commonly taught by guidance teachers are SPHE (20 per cent), LCVP link modules (18 per cent), English (17 per cent) and Religious Education (16 per cent). Guidance Counsellors teach for an average of 9.7 hours a week. As can be observed from Figure 3.3, a considerable proportion of the Guidance Counsellors that reported teaching commitments teach between 9 and 12 hours a week. However, over a third reported teaching for more than twelve hours a week; in other words, this group was allocated some guidance hours but spent the bulk of their time on subject teaching.

Guidance Counsellors in smaller schools were significantly more likely to report that they have teaching commitments (84-85 per cent in schools with fewer than 600 students compared with 67 per cent in schools with 600 or more pupils). There were no significant differences between school sectors, fee paying and non-fee paying schools, or by designated disadvantaged status in terms of whether the Guidance Counsellor has any teaching commitments. However, those not taking part in the GEI were significantly more likely to have teaching commitments than those in the GEI (82 per cent of those not in the GEI compared to 52 per cent of those in the GEI). As well as being more likely to have teaching commitments, Guidance Counsellors in smaller schools also tended to teach longer hours than those in larger schools (see Table 3.1). There were no significant differences between school types, fee paying and non-fee paying status, designated disadvantaged status or participation in the GEI in terms of the number of weekly hours that Guidance Counsellors spend teaching.

Table 3.1: Weekly hours spent teaching subjects by school size

School Size	Mean Hours Teaching
Less than 250 students	13.1
250-499 students	9.5
500-799 students	8.6
800+ students	6.1
Total	9.7

If attention is confined to non-guidance-related teaching only (that is, to teaching "academic" subjects), 60 per cent of Guidance Counsellors are found to have at least some involvement in subject teaching. The pattern varies across types of schools with Guidance Counsellors in larger schools, GEI schools and the community/comprehensive sector being less likely to be involved in subject teaching.

Three-quarters of the Guidance Counsellors who have teaching hours reported that it was difficult to balance time between their teaching and guidance commitments. Not surprisingly, there is a relationship between number of hours taught and difficulty combining teaching and guidance. However, the majority of all those spending more than three hours per week teaching report such difficulties.

Among all Guidance Counsellors (whether teaching or not), an alarming four-fifths of Guidance Counsellors reported that their current time allocation is not sufficient for their guidance-related activities and that they had to use non-guidance time for some tasks. A perceived difficulty in carrying out guidance-related tasks within the allocated time was evident across all types and sizes of school. However, Guidance Counsellors in schools that were participating in the Guidance Enhancement Initiative (GEI) were significantly more positive about being able to address guidance issues within the allocated time (39 per cent of Guidance Counsellors in the GEI compared to 18 per cent of Guidance Counsellors not in the GEI).

The vast majority (88 per cent) of the Guidance Counsellors surveyed also reported that they would like to have more time for guidance-related activities. Those in schools not participating in the GEI were more likely to report needing more time for guidance (90 per cent compared with 72 per cent). A similar proportion (90 per cent) agreed that their school needs more time allocated for guidance. The need for a greater guidance allocation was reported across all school types and sizes, indicating widespread difficulties with addressing guidance issues within the current time allocation. The extra allocation of resources associated with participation in the GEI appeared to make a difference since Guidance Counsellors in GEI schools were less likely to feel their school needs more time allocated for guidance than those in non-GEI schools (78 per cent compared with 92 per cent). However, it should be noted that, even in GEI schools, over three-quarters of guidance personnel felt extra guidance resources were needed.

3.4 NATURE OF GUIDANCE ACTIVITIES AND INVOLVEMENT

3.4.1 Guidance Counsellor involvement in range of activities

An important focus of the questionnaire was the role played by Guidance Counsellors in second-level schools and the kinds of activities in which they are engaged. Providing careers-related guidance emerged as the single most important activity undertaken by guidance personnel with 95 per cent of Guidance Counsellors reporting that providing careers guidance was an important or very important Guidance Counsellor activity (see Figure 3.4). Furthermore, four-fifths of guidance personnel mentioned academic guidance as an important part of their role while 88 per cent deemed personal and social guidance as very important or important. The strong focus of the Guidance Counsellor role on career guidance, academic support and personal/social guidance is in keeping with the perceptions of school Principals in Chapter Two.

A number of other activities were mentioned by a relatively high proportion of Guidance Counsellors; these included evaluating the school's guidance needs (88 per cent), consultation with parents (86 per cent) and carrying out ability testing (80 per cent). Assisting in the transfer from primary to secondary school was rated by two-thirds of Guidance Counsellors as one of their important activities while just under two-thirds (61 per cent) also rated organising subject choices as important. Activities which Guidance Counsellors were less likely to consider as important parts of their role were dealing with work experience (51 per cent), assisting non-national students (48 per cent) and assisting students from Traveller families (33 per cent).

Career, academic and personal/social guidance were seen as central to the role of Guidance Counsellor across all types of school. However, some variation between schools was evident in relation to other activities. Guidance Counsellors in designated disadvantaged schools were more likely to rate dealing with work experience as an important activity, a pattern that is due to the greater number of programmes (such as LCA) involving work experience in these schools. Guidance Counsellors in larger schools, schools with designated disadvantaged status and schools taking part in the GEI were significantly more likely to rate assisting with the transfer from primary to secondary school as an important or very important Guidance Counsellor activity. Guidance Counsellors in larger schools were more likely to mention assisting minority groups (non-national and Traveller students) as an important activity while assisting Traveller students was also seen as an important activity in designated disadvantaged schools and, to some extent, schools participating in the GEI.

Figure 3.4: Main activities of Guidance Counsellors

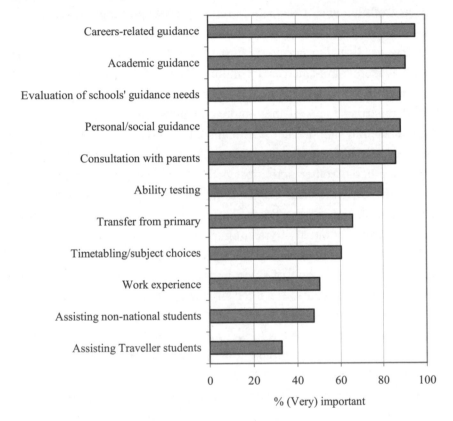

When the Guidance Counsellors were asked what they considered to be the single most important activity in relation to their role as Guidance Counsellor, providing careers-related advice was mentioned in 57 per cent of cases. Providing personal and social guidance (29 per cent) and providing academic guidance (19 per cent) were the other two most important activities listed by Guidance Counsellors.

The single most important activity mentioned by Guidance Counsellors appears to reflect the resource allocation to schools along with the

nature of the student cohort. Careers-related guidance was more frequently deemed the most important activity in very small schools (74 per
cent in schools with under 250 students compared with 59 per cent in
schools with more than 800 students), indicating that, in the context of
scarce resources, careers guidance tends to be given priority. Similarly,
variation was evident across school sectors: Guidance Counsellors in
community/comprehensive schools were most likely, and those in boys'
secondary schools least likely, to name personal/social guidance as their
most important activity (48 per cent compared with 20 per cent).

The additional resources provided to GEI schools appears to have
enabled these schools to broaden their focus beyond careers guidance; 61
per cent of Guidance Counsellors in non-GEI schools rated career guidance as their most important activity compared with 38 per cent of those
in GEI schools. Interesting differences also emerge according to whether
the Guidance Counsellor describes themselves as the main person responsible for guidance in the school. Those who are not the main person
are much more likely to name their main activity as personal/social
counselling (44 per cent compared with 25 per cent of the "main" guidance teachers) and much less likely to report their main activity as careers-related guidance (28 per cent compared with 67 per cent). They are
also more likely to describe their role as a "contact point for students"
(20 per cent compared with 3 per cent).

The role of the Guidance Counsellor is also found to be influenced
by the nature of the student cohort and perceived student needs. Thus,
providing personal/social and academic guidance were mentioned more
frequently in designated disadvantaged schools while careers-related
guidance was mentioned more often in non-disadvantaged schools.

3.4.2 Timetabled classes with different year groups

Guidance Counsellors were asked if they had timetabled classes with the
different year groups, and the frequency of such classes (see Table 3.2).
Two-thirds had weekly timetabled classes with Leaving Certificate (Established) and Leaving Certificate Applied groups, while 64 per cent reported that they had weekly timetabled classes with Transition Years.
Just under half had weekly timetabled classes with Leaving Certificate

Vocational Programme classes. Timetabled classes were far less prevalent amongst the junior cycle classes. Only 15 per cent of Guidance
Counsellors had weekly timetabled classes with Junior Certificate year
classes, and just 7 per cent had classes with first years. Those in girls'
secondary schools were somewhat more likely than those in other school
sectors to have timetabled classes with junior cycle students, although
the difference between school types was not significant; over a third of
Guidance Counsellors in girls' secondary schools had at least occasional
timetabled classes with first year students compared with a tenth of those
in boys' schools. The proportion of Guidance Counsellors who had PLC
or adult education classes was small: fewer than 1 per cent had weekly
timetabled classes with adult classes (such as VTOS) while 8 per cent
had regular classes with PLC students.

Table 3.2: Timetabled classes with different year groups

Year Group	Timetabled Classes?		
	No (%)	Yes, Occa-sionally (%)	Yes, Weekly (%)
First Year	79.3	13.3	7.4
Junior Certificate Year	65.5	19.8	14.7
Transition Year*	26.5	9.9	63.6
Leaving Certificate Established	26.6	6.4	67.0
Leaving Certificate Applied (LCA)*	26.6	4.5	68.9
Leaving Certificate Vocational (LCVP)*	48.9	7.0	44.1
Post-Leaving Certificate (PLC)	89.4	2.6	8.0
Adult classes (incl. VTOS)	99.3	0	0.7
Other (2nd years and 5th years)	84.9	1.8	13.3

Note: * Figures are based on proportions within schools providing these programmes.
This cannot be calculated in the same way for PLC and adult education classes due to
missing information at the school level.

3.4.3 Working with individuals in different year groups

The two main groups that Guidance Counsellors reported working with, on an individual basis, were Leaving Certificate classes and Junior Certificate classes. In total, 87 per cent of Guidance Counsellors reported working with individuals in their Leaving Certificate (Established) Year. Among those working in schools providing the programmes, 79 per cent worked with individuals in the LCA programme while 71 per cent worked with LCVP students. Within schools providing Transition Year, four-fifths of Guidance Counsellors reported working with individuals taking the programme. Three-quarters of Guidance Counsellors reported working with individuals in their Junior Certificate year. In contrast to the other second-level year groups, Guidance Counsellors were less likely to work with first years (61 per cent). In terms of post-second-level provision, a quarter of Guidance Counsellors worked with individuals in PLC courses with 4 per cent working with individuals in adult education classes.

There was significant variation across different types of schools in the extent to which Guidance Counsellors worked with junior cycle students, especially those in first year. To a large extent, working with junior cycle students appears to be related to the level of resources allocated to the school for guidance purposes. Thus, Guidance Counsellors in larger schools are much more likely to work with individual first year students; 82 per cent of those in very large (800+) schools work with first years compared with 28 per cent of those in very small (<250) schools. Similarly, Guidance Counsellors in GEI schools are significantly more likely to work with first years (81 per cent compared with 57 per cent of those in non-GEI schools). Those in designated disadvantaged schools are also somewhat more likely to deal with first years (69 per cent compared with 57 per cent in non-disadvantaged schools).

The pattern in relation to working with Junior Certificate students is similar, although between-school differences are somewhat less marked in nature. Guidance Counsellors in larger schools, GEI schools and designated disadvantaged schools tend to be more likely to work with individual Junior Certificate students. Variation by school sector is also evident with those in community/comprehensive and girls' schools being more likely, and those in vocational schools less likely, to work with Junior Certificate students.

Guidance Counsellors were asked what proportion of their time they spend with the different year groups. The figures are based on all Guidance Counsellors who provided complete information on their time allocation, regardless of whether their school provides certain programmes. A total of 45 per cent of the Guidance Counsellor's time is spent with Leaving Certificate Established students, 10 per cent with Junior Certificate students, 12 per cent with LCVP students, 10 per cent with Transition Year students, 8 per cent with LCA students, 6 per cent with First Years, 4 per cent with PLC students, 1 per cent with adult classes and 2 per cent with other student groups.

In keeping with the patterns above, variation across schools is evident in the time allocated to junior cycle students. Guidance Counsellors in community/comprehensive schools, larger schools and schools with designated disadvantaged status tend to spend relatively more of their time on first year and Junior Certificate students than those in other school types. In keeping with the stated objective of the initiative, involvement in GEI is found to facilitate a greater allocation of time to junior cycle students (see Figure 3.5).

Figure 3.5: Proportion of time allocated to junior cycle students by GEI status

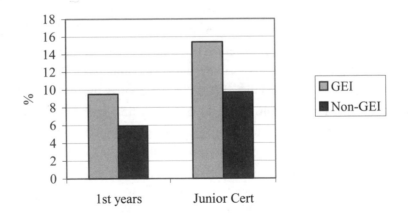

3.4.4 Guidance Counsellors' involvement in specific guidance activities

Guidance Counsellors were asked to state their level of involvement in a range of specific school activities: relating to the allocation of students to classes, the choice of subjects, advising students on their post-school plans and assistance with students' personal problems.

1. Assisting in allocation of students to classes

In around two-thirds of cases, Guidance Counsellors surveyed report that they (or another Guidance Counsellor in the school) are the main person or a significant person in allocating students to Leaving Certificate Established and LCVP classes. Over half are the significant or main person in allocating students to first year, Junior Certificate and LCA classes. Only a minority of Guidance Counsellors are not involved in class allocation; this is more likely to be the case in relation to junior cycle class groups. Where Guidance Counsellors were not the main person involved, the Principal was cited as the main person involved in 42 per cent of cases. Also mentioned were the Year Head(s) (27 per cent) and the Deputy Principal (11 per cent).

Table 3.3: Assisting in allocation of students to classes

Are You?	1st year %	JC %	LCE %	LCA* %	LCVP* %
Main person involved	33.8	31.4	43.6	37.5	45.3
Significant but not main	23.8	24.1	23.4	20.4	19.4
Minor involvement	18.8	18.0	15.1	26.0	24.7
Not involved	23.5	26.5	17.8	16.2	10.6

Note: * Figures are based on proportions within schools providing these programmes.

2. Deciding the number and kind of subjects offered to students in the school

Only just over a tenth of Guidance Counsellors said Guidance Counsellors were the main people involved in deciding the number and kind of subjects offered to students in the school. The most common pattern (ex-

cept in relation to the LCA group) was for Guidance Counsellors to say
they were a significant, but not the main, person. Between a quarter and
a third of Guidance Counsellors described themselves as not at all involved in deciding on subject provision. Where the Guidance Counsellor
was not the main person involved, the Principal was the main person
named in over two-thirds of cases.

*Table 3.4: Deciding the number and kind of subjects offered to
students in the school*

Are You . . .?	1st year %	JC %	LCE %	LCA* %	LCVP* %
Main person involved	13.8	14.5	12.4	13.3	15.4
Significant but not main	37.2	40.7	50.8	31.8	36.4
Minor involvement	20.3	16.5	13.4	16.5	12.8
Not involved	28.7	28.3	23.4	38.4	35.4

Note: * Figures are based on proportions within schools providing these programmes.

3. Advising and helping students regarding choice of subjects

Guidance Counsellors tend to describe themselves as the main person
involved in advising students on subject choice, especially in relation to
the Leaving Certificate Established group. The figure is somewhat lower
for first year students; in 59 per cent of cases, Guidance Counsellors are
the main people involved compared with 86 per cent for LCE students.
This pattern may relate to the timing of subject choice in the school (see
Chapter Two). It appears Guidance Counsellors play a strong role in advising students on their subject choices, although their role in decisions
regarding the range of subjects to be offered to students is more variable.
Where the Guidance Counsellors were not the main person, the most
frequently mentioned personnel were the Principal (47 per cent), the
Year Heads (15 per cent) and the Deputy Principal (11 per cent).

Table 3.5: Advising and helping students regarding choice of subjects

Are You?	1st year %	JC %	LCE %	LCA* %	LCVP* %
Main person involved	59.7	72.1	86.1	64.4	67.8
Significant but not main	16.2	13.6	11.2	15.9	17.8
Minor involvement	9.9	6.2	1.9	7.8	6.4
Not involved	14.1	8.1	0.8	11.9	8.0

Note: * Figures are based on proportions within schools providing these programmes.

4. Advising students regarding choice of career/jobs on leaving school

The majority of Guidance Counsellors said they (or another Guidance Counsellor in the school) were the main person involved in advising students on their choice of careers on leaving school across all of the year groups specified. In the case of first year students, however, almost a tenth reported no involvement of Guidance Counsellors in giving advice on careers. Of the roles examined in this section, it appears vocational/career advice is the area where Guidance Counsellors are most likely to play a strong role. In the small number of cases where the Guidance Counsellor was not the main person involved, Principals tended to be the main people involved in career advice.

Table 3.6: Advising students regarding choice of career/jobs on leaving school

Are You?	1st year %	JC %	LCE %	LCA* %	LCVP* %
Main person involved	84.6	85.3	98.1	87.3	86.1
Significant but not main	6.0	10.8	1.9	8.9	10.0
Minor involvement	0.0	3.1	0.0	1.4	1.4
Not involved	9.4	0.9	0.0	2.4	2.5

Note: * Figures are based on proportions within schools providing these programmes.

3.4.5 Dealing with students' personal problems

Around half of Guidance Counsellors described themselves as the main person involved in dealing with students' personal problems with around a third saying they played a significant, but not the main, role (Table 3.7). Fewer than a tenth of Guidance Counsellors are not at all involved in dealing with students' personal problems. Where the Guidance Counsellor was not the main person involved, the main people mentioned were the Year Head (28 per cent), Chaplain (11 per cent) and the Class Tutor(s) (11 per cent); only 8 per cent mentioned a designated counsellor or psychologist.

Table 3.7: Dealing with students' personal problems

Are You?	1st year %	JC %	LCE %	LCA* %	LCVP* %
Main person involved	50.4	47.6	54.6	50.6	50.7
Significant but not main	28.3	31.8	30.1	35.6	35.7
Minor involvement	15.9	15.2	11.9	6.6	6.9
Not involved	5.4	5.4	3.4	7.2	6.6

Note: * Figures are based on proportions within schools providing these programmes.

3.4.6 Proportion of time spent on broad guidance areas

Guidance Counsellors in all types of schools spent the largest proportion of their time on careers-related guidance (45 per cent). They spent almost a quarter of their time on personal guidance, a fifth on academic guidance and over a tenth on other activities such as administration and meetings with staff. There were no significant differences in the time allocation of Guidance Counsellors by school type (see Figure 3.6). However, those in community/comprehensive schools tended to spend somewhat less time on academic guidance and more time on personal guidance than those in secondary or vocational schools.

Figure 3.6: Proportion of time spent on broad guidance areas

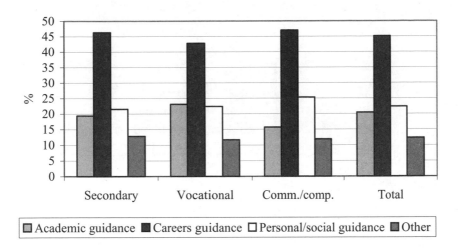

The allocation of time to the three activities is found to reflect differences in guidance resources across schools. Schools with more time allocated to guidance appear to facilitate a greater proportion of time devoted to personal/social guidance. Thus, Guidance Counsellors in large schools spend about twice as much of their time on counselling as those in small schools (27-28 per cent among those in schools with more than 500 students compared with 14 per cent in smaller schools). Differences are also evident according to GEI participation with guidance teachers in GEI schools spending 34 per cent of their time on personal guidance compared with an average of 20 per cent in non-GEI schools. The allocation of time also reflects the nature of the student cohort; Guidance Counsellors in designated disadvantaged schools spent significantly less time on average on careers guidance and significantly more time on personal guidance and other activities than those in non-disadvantaged schools (see Figure 3.7).

Figure 3.7: Time allocation on guidance areas by disadvantaged status

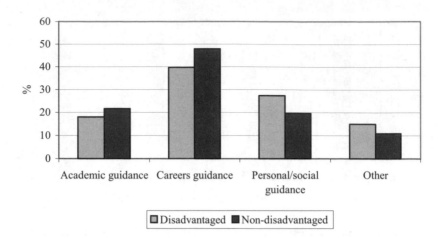

3.5 SATISFACTION WITH GUIDANCE PROVISION

3.5.1 Guidance Counsellors' opinions on the attitudes and capabilities of students in the school

The vast majority (80 per cent) of Guidance Counsellors either strongly agreed or agreed with the statement "students have a good idea how to apply for college". Three-quarters of Guidance Counsellors agreed with the statement that "students have a good idea how to apply for jobs". Furthermore, the majority of Guidance Counsellors (62 per cent) disagree with the statement "students have low aspirations when it comes to thinking about college".

The majority of Guidance Counsellors across all types of schools thought that students in their school had "a good idea of how to apply for jobs" and "have a good idea how to apply for college". However, Guidance Counsellors in designated disadvantaged schools were significantly more likely to agree with the statement that students have low aspirations when it comes to thinking about their future (40 per cent compared with 15 per cent of those in non-disadvantaged schools). Furthermore, those in GEI schools were more likely to feel that their students had low aspirations than those in non-GEI schools (54 per cent compared with 19 per cent).

3.5.2 Guidance Counsellors' views regarding resources, guidance services and staff views

Guidance Counsellors were asked to what extent they agreed with a number of statements regarding guidance provision in their school. Interestingly, 85 per cent of Guidance Counsellors surveyed agreed or strongly agreed that there were some students that are missing out on guidance and counselling that they need; this was higher than the corresponding figure for school Principals (see Chapter Two). In addition, only 30 per cent felt that there were sufficient resources for the Guidance Counsellor's work in the school and almost a third (30 per cent) agreed that there is insufficient appreciation of guidance and counselling among the staff (see Figure 3.8). While Guidance Counsellors expressed some concerns about the adequacy of guidance provision, on the other hand, the majority felt they were involved in policy making in the guidance area (82 per cent), felt that all students could avail of guidance/counselling services if necessary (70 per cent) and felt that their school had a well-developed pastoral care system (64 per cent).

There is some variation across schools in the perceived adequacy of guidance resources and general support structures. Those in designated disadvantaged schools are less likely to feel that there are sufficient resources for the Guidance Counsellor's work in the school (19 per cent compared with 35 per cent in non-disadvantaged schools). On average, Guidance Counsellors in very small schools (less than 250 pupils) were somewhat less likely to agree with the statement "all students in the school can avail of the guidance and counselling services, when necessary". Those in fee-paying secondary schools are less likely than those in other school types to report that "some students are missing out on the guidance and counselling they need". Guidance Counsellors in community/comprehensive schools, larger schools (>600 students), schools with designated disadvantaged status and those in the GEI were on average significantly more likely to agree that "the school has a well-developed pastoral care system" compared to other types of schools. Within the secondary sector, those in boys' schools were least likely to agree with the statement.

Figure 3.8: Views of Guidance Counsellors regarding resources, guidance services and staff views

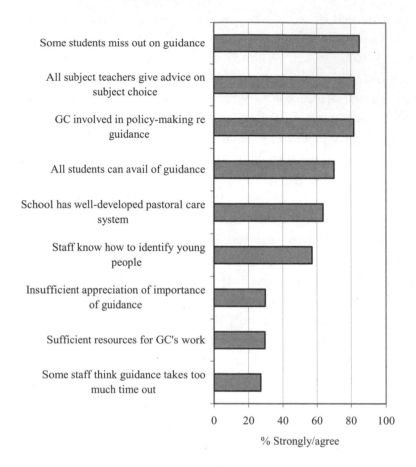

Variation was also evident in perceptions regarding the extent to which guidance was seen as a whole school issue. Guidance Counsellors in GEI schools were significantly more likely to agree with the statement "all staff know how to identify young people who need specialist guidance and advice from the school's Guidance Counsellor" (79 compared with 54 per cent). Those in designated disadvantaged schools were more likely than those in non-disadvantaged schools to feel that they were involved in policy making in the guidance area (90 per cent compared with 78 per cent). A difference was also evident between GEI and non-GEI schools in this respect (93 per cent compared with 80 per cent). In contrast, Guidance Counsellors in boys' secondary schools were less likely to feel involved in policy making and more than twice as likely as those in other school types to consider that there is insufficient appreciation of the importance of guidance and counselling among school staff.

3.5.3 Satisfaction with guidance services

Generally, Guidance Counsellors were satisfied or very satisfied with the guidance services their school was able to provide. Nine out of ten were (very) satisfied with vocational and careers guidance in the school and similarly 89 per cent were (very) satisfied with academic guidance in the school. Guidance Counsellors were not as satisfied with personal/social guidance and counselling (59 per cent), which indicates a gap between the perceived adequacy of careers/academic guidance provision and social/personal guidance provision.

The vast majority of Guidance Counsellors across all types of schools were satisfied with careers guidance in their school. However, differences between schools emerged in relation to the other guidance areas. Those in vocational schools were significantly less satisfied with academic guidance than those in secondary or community/ comprehensive schools (see Figure 3.9). Those in smaller schools were on average less satisfied with academic and personal guidance compared to those in larger schools. Those in disadvantaged schools were somewhat more satisfied than those in non-disadvantaged schools with personal guidance in their school (67 per cent compared with 54 per cent); a similar difference was found between counsellors in GEI and non-GEI schools (73 per cent compared with 57 per cent). However, those in fee-paying secondary schools were more satisfied with personal and academic guidance than those in other school types.

Figure 3.9: Satisfaction with guidance services by school type

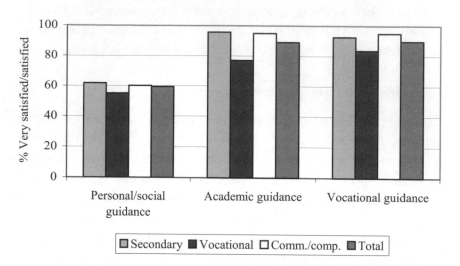

Guidance Counsellors were asked to indicate how satisfied they were with the contribution of the guidance service in their school in seven more specific areas. Four-fifths of Guidance Counsellors were (very) satisfied with the provision of specialist advice and guidance to *individual* young people. Guidance Counsellors were not as satisfied with the provision of specialist advice and guidance to *groups* of young people (60 per cent). In total, 71 per cent were satisfied that the service was responding flexibly to changing career guidance advice needs in the school. In addition, 73 per cent were satisfied that the service was identifying the students most in need of specialist advice (either from within or outside the school).

Areas where Guidance Counsellors were not as satisfied included the way the service was providing feedback to management or staff regarding careers and counselling (55 per cent were satisfied), monitoring the career progress of young people on leaving school (only 36 per cent were satisfied) and training teachers in identifying young people in need of specialist advice (only 22 per cent were satisfied).

Guidance Counsellors in designated disadvantaged schools and schools that were taking part in the GEI were significantly more satisfied that the service was identifying the students most in need of specialist advice. Satisfaction with the provision of specialist advice to individual young people was higher in community/comprehensive and girls' secondary schools than in other school types. Satisfaction also varied by school size with all schools with 800 or more pupils being satisfied, 77 per cent in schools with 500 to 799 pupils, 86 per cent in schools with 250 to 499 pupils and only 64 per cent in schools with less than 250 pupils. Satisfaction with advice to individual young people was also higher in designated disadvantaged schools than in non-disadvantaged schools. Dissatisfaction with feedback to, and training of, staff, and the monitoring of young people after leaving school was evident across all types of schools, indicating a widespread gap in provision in these areas.

3.5.4 Written guidance plan

Two-thirds of Guidance Counsellors reported that their school had no written guidance plan. Fee-paying secondary schools are significantly more likely on average to have a written guidance plan (73 per cent of fee-paying schools compared to 31 per cent of non-fee paying secondary schools). Schools participating in the GEI were also more likely to have a written guidance plan (52 per cent of schools in the GEI compared to 31 per cent of schools not in the GEI). There were no significant differences on the basis of school size, designated disadvantaged status or school type. Where a guidance plan was in place in the schools, the Guidance Counsellor was involved in 90 per cent of cases with the Principal involved in 61 per cent of cases.

Interestingly, having a written guidance plan in place in the schools is associated with higher satisfaction levels with personal guidance, academic guidance and careers guidance (see Figure 3.10), though this may reflect a greater whole school commitment to guidance in these cases rather than the existence of a written plan *per se*. With the exception of the provision of specialist advice and guidance to groups of young people, having a written guidance plan is also significantly associated with higher satisfaction with provision in specific guidance areas (see Figure 3. 11).

Figure 3.10: Satisfaction with guidance services by written guidance plan

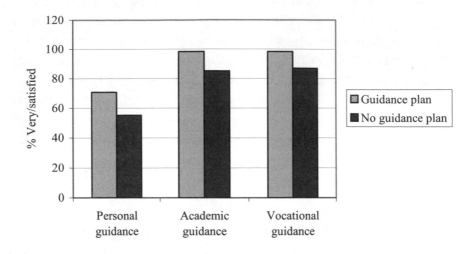

Figure 3.11: Satisfaction with specific guidance areas by guidance plan

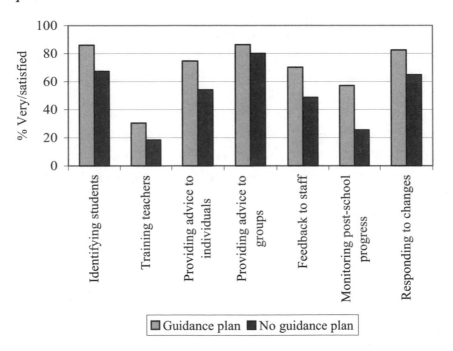

Almost two-thirds of Guidance Counsellors described themselves as involved to a great extent in deciding the direction of guidance-related policy and practice in their school; a fifth said they were involved to some extent, 7 per cent said they were not involved to any great extent while 7 per cent said they were not involved to any extent. As might be expected, those who were not the main guidance person in the school described themselves as less involved in policy direction (37 per cent were involved to a great extent compared with 72 per cent of those who were the main person). Over two-thirds (71 per cent) of Guidance Counsellors stated they would like to be more involved in the development of school policy in the guidance area. As might be expected, those who were currently less involved were more likely to state they would like more involvement.

3.5.5 Professional development and training

A total of 54 per cent of Guidance Counsellors reported that they had received guidance-related training in the twelve months prior to the survey. Those in vocational schools were somewhat less likely to have received such training than those in the other school types, although the differences between school sectors were not highly significant. Guidance Counsellors in smaller schools were significantly less likely to have received any guidance-related training in the previous year (22 per cent of those in schools with fewer than 250 students compared with 71 per cent of those in schools with more than 800 students). Participation in in-service training did not vary significantly by disadvantaged status, participation in the GEI or whether the Guidance Counsellor was the main person involved in guidance. Where Guidance Counsellors took part in training, the most frequently attended courses were Institute of Guidance Counsellors in-service courses (18 per cent), training in a specific counselling technique (17 per cent) and computer/other IT courses (10 per cent).

Overwhelmingly, 91 per cent of Guidance Counsellors stated that they would be interested in further guidance-related training. Those working in larger schools were more likely to say they would be interested in further training, although the majority across all sizes of schools expressed such an interest. Interest in further training did not vary significantly by school type, disadvantaged status or whether the respondent was the main guidance person. Those in GEI schools were somewhat more likely than those in non-GEI schools to express an interest in training. When asked about the kinds of areas they would be interested in, interest was greatest in relation to counselling (36 per cent), student assessment and testing (29 per cent) and computer/IT courses (11 per cent).

When Guidance Counsellors were asked how easy they found it to participate in available guidance-related training, the majority (62 per cent) said that it is sometimes difficult to find time to attend courses. Over a fifth (22 per cent) said they can always attend courses and 16 per cent said they could never find time to attend courses. The perceived difficulty in attending courses did not vary according to school characteristics. However, as might be expected, those with teaching commitments found it more difficult to find the time to attend courses.

3.5.6 Strengths and weaknesses of guidance provision

Guidance Counsellors were asked about the main strengths and weaknesses of guidance provision in their school along with areas of guidance they would like to develop in the future. The main strengths mentioned were their availability to, and individual contact with, students (30 per cent), a whole school approach with support from management and staff (24 per cent) and the commitment and enthusiasm of the guidance personnel (22 per cent). The main weaknesses mentioned were insufficient hours allocated to guidance (47 per cent) and lack of time specifically allocated to counselling (17 per cent). Priorities for future development included counselling (18 per cent), having a guidance plan (12 per cent), provision for junior cycle students (11 per cent) and more guidance hours (10 per cent).

3.6 SUMMARY AND DISCUSSION

The core activities of Guidance Counsellors are found to centre on career guidance, academic guidance and, to a somewhat lesser extent, personal/social support and counselling. The central role of the Guidance Counsellor tends to reflect the resources available to individual schools. The additional resources allocated to larger schools and to schools involved in the GEI enables these schools to broaden their focus beyond careers guidance towards a greater emphasis on personal support and counselling. The role of the Guidance Counsellor is also found to be influenced by the nature of student intake to the school with a greater emphasis on personal/social support and academic guidance in designated disadvantaged schools.

Guidance Counsellor involvement currently centres mainly on the senior cycle class groups based on timetabled classes, work with individual students and the proportion of time allocated. However, some schools have a greater focus than others on students in the junior cycle. This focus tends to reflect greater resources with Guidance Counsellors having a greater involvement with junior cycle, especially first year, students in large schools and those participating in the GEI.

Variation between schools is also evident in the formal integration of guidance into the school structures and satisfaction with guidance provision. On the whole, Guidance Counsellors do not feel there are sufficient resources for their work and most report difficulties dealing with guidance activities within their allocated time. As was reported by Principals, the majority of Guidance Counsellors report having no written guidance plan in the school, although most Guidance Counsellors feel they have an input into deciding policy in the area of guidance. Satisfaction with guidance provision tends to be higher in schools with a formal guidance policy. In terms of informal structures and climate, a significant minority of Guidance Counsellors feel that staff are not able to identify "at risk" students for referral and consider that guidance is not sufficiently appreciated by other staff, indicating the lack of a whole school approach to guidance in a significant number of schools.

In terms of the professional identity of Guidance Counsellors, the majority of Guidance Counsellors are combining their guidance role with non-guidance related teaching, leading to difficulties in juggling the two roles. Four-fifths of Guidance Counsellors have formal guidance qualifications, although such qualifications are less prevalent among those in smaller schools. There is a strong interest in taking part in further training among Guidance Counsellors, principally in relation to counselling, student assessment and computer studies.

Findings from the survey indicate some important variations in opinion both within and across schools, variations which are more fully explored in the case study analysis in Chapters Four to Seven.

Chapter Four

GUIDANCE PROVISION IN THE
CASE STUDY SCHOOLS

4.1 INTRODUCTION

This chapter is the first of four chapters presenting findings from in-depth interviews conducted in the fifteen case study schools. These chapters presenting "qualitative" information on the schools take the following format. Chapter Four examines the nature of guidance and support services for students in the schools, based on the reports of key personnel. Among the areas considered are the nature of pastoral care supports in the schools, the level of guidance provision, participation in the GEI, the role played by Guidance Counsellors, the time spent with different year groups and Leaving Certificate programmes, the links with the curriculum and the extent of contact with parents. Chapter Five explores students' own views of the guidance they have received and the nature of supports they feel are available to them in school. Chapter Six looks at a number of central issues emerging in schools: the extent to which schools adopt a whole school approach to guidance and student support, the role of schools in personal/social support and counselling, the wider external support services, the professional identity of Guidance Counsellors and training issues. Finally Chapter Seven considers variations across schools in the structure and nature of guidance and support services for students. In addition, the chapter outlines key personnel evaluations of the guidance services in their schools, including the perceived strengths, weaknesses and priorities for the future development of guidance. Chapter Eight discusses the findings and draws out some implications for policy and practice.

4.2 PASTORAL CARE STRUCTURES

4.2.1 Pastoral care system

The case study schools varied somewhat in the nature of the pastoral care in place for students. In line with other studies (see Smyth *et al.*, 2004, for example), nearly all of the schools had a Tutor and Year Head system in place. However, schools varied somewhat in the extent to which additional supports were made available to students. Additional pastoral care personnel and programmes were available in a number of the schools. These included mentor/buddy systems, homework and breakfast clubs and key personnel such as religious education teachers and Chaplains taking a central role. Trained counsellors, as well as Guidance Counsellors, also play an important role in a number of the schools, which is discussed in the next section focusing on guidance provision.

The roles of Year Head and Tutor were distinct positions which, in many cases, reflected a distinction between disciplinary and pastoral roles: in many schools the Year Head would take a more disciplinarian role while the Tutors would be somewhat more supportive of the students and would refer them to the Year Head in the event of discipline/behaviour issues:

> We have the Year Head [who] is more of a disciplinarian. The students don't talk to a disciplinarian on that more supportive pastoral level. (Principal, Riverbank)

Half of the case study schools also had a Chaplain post, which many considered central in the holistic support of students and the pastoral care structures in general:

> Yes, [the Chaplain is] probably *the* key person. Working along side the Year Heads, Tutors, Guidance Counsellor, those who have posts that are related to pastoral care, health and safety, those who have posts for learning difficulties. (Chaplain, Riverbank)

For example, the Chaplain in Riverbank school noted having a ". . . particular concern for students who are living with some kind of difficulty. Students who are emotionally not well. Students who have family issues.

Students who are bereaved, separated parents. Students who are in crisis".

While the Chaplain was often seen to work with all year groups, in some cases their work was more targeted at first years, which seems to counter the pre-dominant focus on senior cycle students by Guidance Counsellors, as discussed later in the chapter:

> [The Chaplain would meet] all the first years at the start of the year. I met them first in their class and introduced myself and said who I was, then I took them in a small group and individually. Maybe just tell me about your family, your home, who else is in the school, anything that worries you about school, very general things, that tells me a lot of things. (Chaplain, Riverbank).

In three schools the Chaplain's post was vacant and this was seen to be creating difficulties in the schools in being able to offer a comprehensive support service to students. The Chaplainry post is vacant in Oakhill Way and Seaview, for example, and in both schools difficulties in filling the position are creating worries regarding the level of pastoral support available to students, as the Guidance Counsellor in one school, for example, does not feel in the position to deal with issues of a more "spiritual" nature:

> I think the absence of a Chaplain is important. I wouldn't feel confident or comfortable with, you know sometimes you have pupils coming in and it is a spiritual matter they want to talk about and I don't feel qualified in that. We are supposed to have a Chaplain but I think it's on the cards to get one. (Guidance Counsellor, Oakhill Way).

In other schools the absence of a Chaplain post is perceived as a weakness and an issue in the availability of non-teacher pastoral support to students. The Principal in Willow Grove, for example, highlighted the importance of a Chaplain who would be ". . . a more neutral person than a class teacher, where their relationship might be affected by what goes on in class".

Outside of the central pastoral care system involving the Guidance Counsellor, Chaplain, Tutors and Year Heads, student or peer support systems are also in place in a number of schools. In Ashton Park, for example, a "buddy" system has recently been introduced with training for senior students acting as "buddies" to younger students:

> [. . .] a leadership programme for fifth years. These are trained to act as leaders for the first years, "buddies" really, for our incoming first years. . . . That is working quite well, then what we do is we link one fifth year with five first years and they meet regularly in the first few weeks. . . . We have found that, in fact, last year they were extremely helpful. (Home School Community Liaison Officer).

Similarly, a mentoring system was also seen as playing an important pastoral role in Chestnut Drive and Greenwood:

> Sixth year repeat pupils . . . one of their roles is as mentor for first year students. And in preparing them for that role the South West Counselling Centre would come out for a number of afternoons at the beginning of the year and give them training. (Principal, Chestnut Drive).

4.2.2 Perceptions of pastoral care provision

Schools varied widely in their perceptions of the adequacy of pastoral care supports for students. Around half of the schools were generally positive about the arrangements in place for pastoral support and felt students were being offered an effective range of supports:

> I think it really works, I have to say, I think we have a really good pastoral system, I don't think much can be improved on it. We have the Year Heads, the Tutors. I think it works very well. (Deputy Principal, Hills Road).

> The pastoral care system is good here now, in fairness the vast majority of the staff are really solidly behind the kids that are in their care in terms of being Tutors, there's very few Tutors who just come and take the roll, a lot of time is taken up . . . by the teachers here and I'm not just saying that . . . there is a huge amount of care and concern for the kids and that's where the pastoral system works best. (Chaplain, Greenwood).

In one school, very small in terms of pupil enrolment, knowing all students and their parents well was seen as an added benefit to the Guidance

Counsellor in identifying and dealing with problems and issues that arose for students:

> I know the students and their backgrounds. I have been involved [with the] kids at sports, so I have a pretty good knowledge of them and understand their difficulties and problems. So I feel that has helped me to deal with them. Also I meet them outside of school so . . . they would ask me about something as quick as they would in school. (Guidance Counsellor, Willow Grove).

The remaining schools were somewhat more negative in their evaluations of pastoral care supports for students. Some of them identified the need for specific additional supports such as a homework club, a mentor system or counselling services, while others regarded further training for staff as necessary.

> I would like to have things like homework clubs, breakfast clubs. Anything that we can provide for a child to help her to feel secure, to be well fed, not to feel different, and to have a happy time with us, any supports like that would be more than welcome. I think a mentor system as well, as in a buddy system, [that] would be good. (Deputy Principal, Beechwood Square).

A number of schools commented on the need for further time for pastoral care: in particular, a number of personnel noted the need for additional time for meeting and planning pastoral care:

> I think what people find more and more as the curriculum becomes squeezed, time becomes very precious and the ability to create meeting time is limited, the chance for serious interaction, serious planning suffers. (Principal, Laurel Park).

An additional concern in a number of schools was the availability of sufficient numbers of staff for pastoral care duties. This was a particular concern in schools where considerable numbers of staff are working on a job-share basis, resulting in an insufficient pool of full-time staff to fulfil pastoral care duties.

> . . . even things like job sharing, but communicating, the way it's structured here the form teacher meets with each class every day. . . . But anything with a job-sharer, they can't do it because they are only

in half time so they wouldn't be there. So we have far less of a pool
of people to do the job. (Guidance Counsellor, Whitefield).

Calls for greater training for all staff in pastoral care issues were echoed
in a number of schools:

> I think some of the subject teachers would feel they want more train-
> ing in that [pastoral care]. (Guidance Counsellor, Oakhill Way).

Some school personnel argued that the effectiveness of staff in a pastoral
dimension was highly related to their suitability for such a role. This
raises questions over the most appropriate procedures for placing staff in
such roles and whether schools have a sufficient pool of staff to allow a
certain amount of self-selection or exclusion in the event an individual
feels they are less suited to such a role.

> Certainly a certain group of teachers need skills in that [pastoral
> care]. Then there is personality . . . one of the students might relate to
> you and not to me, depending on who you are. All the training in the
> world won't change that. (Principal, Riverbank).

> The pastoral care system is basically as effective as that teacher is in
> that role. Some people fit very naturally into that role and are very
> comfortable with it. (Guidance Counsellor, Willow Grove).

As mentioned earlier, a number of personnel commented on the conflict
teachers and Tutors experience between their teaching commitment, a
role as a disciplinarian, and, on the other hand, the more supportive and
caring dimension of their position. This is a prominent issue in schools
and one which appears to have no simple solution. If teachers are at-
tempting to create an orderly classroom environment most conducive to
learning, can they realistically expect the same students to approach
them with personal issues? Conflict between different roles is evident in
both the national data and focus groups with students in the case study
schools, discussed in Chapter Five. Focus group interviews with students
showed that students find it difficult to approach teachers with personal
issues and would prefer a separation between the roles of counsellor and
teacher, considering it easier to talk openly to someone who was not a
teacher. Such views were further echoed in national data indicating a

strong reliance among young people on non-school sources of advice, particularly the advice of their parents.

> I don't know how efficient it is [the Tutor system] . . . are they using it? They don't seem to be using it enough. The problem I reckon is the teacher teaching them there maybe a conflict in the class and then they are not going to go to them if they have a problem. (Guidance Counsellor, Rosendale).

In line with student views, key personnel also suggested that having staff apart from the regular teaching staff, such as the Guidance Counsellor and Chaplain, was seen as particularly important in providing support to students by staff members who are not viewed as "teachers":

> They are beginning to realise there is another source there, a teacher that is not teaching them that they can go to. I think the Guidance Counsellor can play a huge role there. Also the Religion teacher can play a role there and they do. And they have SPHE and CSPE teachers, they do seem to play a role there. (Guidance Counsellor, Rosendale).

Finally, while most described their pastoral care structures as hierarchical structures often heavily focused on discipline and dealing with behavioural problems, one Deputy Principal identified the need for a greater emphasis on the positive reinforcement aspect of pastoral care:

> . . . we do need to concentrate on [the] positive and not just the negative or the small group of difficult students . . . the Tutor should be there as well to see where someone is doing well and to give you know, give a boost there, try and promote that side and give incentives. (Deputy Principal, Cherryfield View).

4.3 LEVEL OF GUIDANCE PROVISION

Apart from the two schools participating in the GEI, just two case study schools (Cherryfield View and Riverbank) expressed any level of satisfaction with the guidance resources received by their school.

> Interviewer: Do you feel the school has sufficient resources for guidance and counselling?

> Guidance Counsellor: I would be inclined to think we have a very
> good service at the moment with what I need, possibly not the best in
> the country, but from that point of view there isn't a problem. (Riv-
> erbank).

For the remaining schools, concerns about the level of funding were vari-
ously expressed. In nearly all cases, schools felt that resources targeted
towards the guidance services were inadequate and unable to adequately
address student needs. This was seen to be particularly important in the
context of wider societal problems and difficulties faced by students in
their social and personal lives. Many Principals and Guidance Counsellors felt that schools had an important preventative role to play and highlighted the longer term cost implications of a failure to address social and
personal problems experienced by students at an early stage.

> Interviewer: Do you think the school has sufficient resources for
> guidance counselling?

> Deputy Principal: No, I think it did, I think it was more or less okay
> 10 years ago when there were fewer numbers in the school and we
> had a Chaplain who was sharing the burden of pastoral care. Now
> with greater numbers and only the Guidance Counsellor it's not
> enough. (Oakhill Way).

> Interviewer: Do you feel the school has sufficient resources with one
> guidance teacher?

> Principal: Oh no, no, sure I mean it's only a tokenism, it really is a
> token, now the school guidance person is free there all the time to
> talk to individuals, students and that, but even if he were to give 10
> minutes to every student in the school over the length of the whole
> year, he'd only meet them once, so it's very little really. (Green-
> wood).

In general, there was strong criticism of the system of allocation of resources and the inflexibility of the quota system.[7]

---

[7] Chapter One details the level of resources targeted at guidance services and the system
of allocation.

> We have another trained counsellor on the staff but because we're
> under a certain magical number from the department she can't oper-
> ate, I think that's crazy and it's immoral in many ways that we have
> somebody on the staff who has the skill to deal with the kids and be-
> cause of the numbers game that we're playing with the department
> we can't offer that service. (Chaplain, Greenwood).

There was little evidence, apart from one school, of underutilisation of
guidance resources. According to the NCGE Audit of 1999–2000, there
was significant under-utilisation by school management of the allocation
given by the Department of Education and Science – this applied in 23
per cent of secondary schools, 25 per cent of community and comprehensive schools and 44 per cent of vocational schools. This did not appear to be an issue among the case study schools. On the contrary, a
number of the schools added to their guidance allocation:

> I think to have to take from our teacher allocation, a half teacher
> equivalent to provide a full-time Guidance Counsellor for our stu-
> dents isn't the way. I think the 500 cut off point is too high. I am not
> completely happy with the situation where I have a very valuable re-
> source like [name of Guidance Counsellor] who could really disap-
> pear [in] the next teacher allocation. It's always subject to an appeal
> to retain it. (Principal, Laurel Park).

Other schools drew on other resources to employ the expertise of specialist counsellors for a number of hours on a weekly basis.

> . . . we have a counsellor that comes in three hours a week. She is [a]
> fully qualified accredited counsellor. She has done the Trinity coun-
> selling course. She has a background in psychology.. . . So we use
> three of those hours [from our special needs allocation] to pay for the
> counselling. So they are not coming out of guidance. (Guidance
> Counsellor, Maplewood).

A number of other schools arranged for private counsellors to come to
their schools, sometimes funded through school resources or else by parents themselves. One of the case study schools avails of third level counselling students seeking work placements. Clearly the need to draw on
other school resources and private sector support raises serious issues
over the level of resources devoted to guidance services in schools and

the capacity of schools to offer a comprehensive and effective guidance and counselling service to all students.

The lack of resources for a number of smaller schools also meant poor guidance facilities.

> Our facilities are dismal. I have stuff stacked up in the staff room, I try to keep it as tidy as I can. I have another batch of it [material] in the Room 8. If somebody comes to me at some time there are classes on there is a difficulty going in to ask them to open the press up. There should be some little room. . . . It's not satisfactory. (Guidance Counsellor, Willow Grove).

The lack of a guidance room also has implications for students' use of the service. In particular, the Guidance Counsellor felt that students are not likely to approach him with issues as they have no place to talk confidentially with him.

Such a lack of facilities was strongly related to school size and only affected the smaller schools in the case study analysis. This is supported by the NCGE (1999/2000) Audit which found that only 10 per cent of schools do not have a dedicated office for guidance work with students and the overall picture with reference to the provision of office, telephone line, computer and internet facilities and access to photocopier, fax, secretarial and administrative support was positive.

Findings from the national survey reveal further variations across schools in the facilities for guidance and counselling. While the survey found that having a guidance room and administrative support for guidance did not vary by school size or disadvantaged status, having access to a private phone, computer and internet facilities was more likely among larger schools. Furthermore, while just one-third of schools report having a designated budget for guidance materials, this was more common in community/comprehensive schools and less common in vocational schools.

4.3.1 Implications of insufficient resources

Ultimately, the shortcomings in resources were invariably reflected in the time allocation for Guidance Counselling:

> We don't get to every student, we look at the list at the end of every
> school year or during it and say we have seen her four times and she
> has missed three appointments or you know, we just don't get to see
> everybody. I do feel guilty. (Guidance Counsellor, Maplewood).

While a strong focus on careers and vocational guidance was seen as a
key strength in many of the schools, the corollary of this is a perceived
neglect of the more student support/counselling aspect of the Guidance
Counsellor's role. With limitations in time and resources, many school
personnel, including Guidance Counsellors, felt they were unable to offer an adequate personal support and counselling role to their students.

> . . . even our Guidance Counsellors they will have so much training
> but then when it comes to the actual allocation of time, the careers
> end of things will sap a lot of that. (Pastoral Care Co-ordinator, Hills
> Road).

> I would see a weakness possibly in the counselling area, that I can't
> sufficiently address. It needs to be addressed now. (Guidance Coun-
> sellor, Riverbank).

While many schools and Guidance Counsellors concentrated attention on
addressing the career guidance needs of students, this was not the case in
all schools. In a number of schools, the lack of guidance time and resources has resulted in priority being given to one-to-one counselling
provision and this has meant reliance on private career guidance for students:

> I know a lot of students go to outside, I don't know if they are career
> guidance teachers, but outside, they seek outside advice. I don't
> know what it is, I suppose they just pay 90 to 100 euro to find out
> what are their strengths. (Deputy Principal, Beechwood Square).

In line with a perceived short-fall in guidance resources, some personnel
also maintained that there was insufficient time for planning and interaction among staff regarding guidance and counselling issues. This seems
particularly important in a context where all schools are required to develop a guidance plan but face the considerable hurdle of finding time
and opportunity to meet regarding such a plan. Given the obvious benefits of having a plan in place and the evidence of a more effective and

satisfactory guidance service in schools which have developed such a plan (see Chapter Three), the issue of staff time to prepare and discuss such plans seems important.

Others pointed to the difficulties in balancing a guidance role with that of a teaching role and argued for the need for a full-time guidance allocation in all schools.

> I think every school should be allocated a full[-time] guidance teacher regardless of the size. Even if you have only thirty in sixth [year], thirty still need to go on to college. You know, and you have fifth years. So I think every school, they should be the same. (Deputy Principal, Cherryfield View).

Earlier research on this issue (O'Leary, 1987; O'Leary and Adams, 1986) suggested that Guidance Counsellors prefer to do some subject teaching in addition to performing their counselling duties, but not as much as they are typically assigned. However, such research was undertaken at a time when there was a greater allocation of guidance to schools and a somewhat lower teaching burden being placed on Guidance Counsellors (typically teaching for five hours a week). Conversely, guidelines issued by the IGC do not perceive subject teaching as part of the Guidance Counsellor's role (1985).

Overall, with varying statutory guidance allocations (largely based on the quota system relating to student numbers – see Chapter One for details), two schools participating in the GEI and a range of other resources being used for guidance purposes, the schools varied widely in their overall guidance personnel (see Table 4.1).

4.4 GUIDANCE ENHANCEMENT INITIATIVE

As discussed in Chapter One, additional resources have been allocated to schools under the Guidance Enhancement Initiative (GEI). To date, such resources have been allocated to over 180 second-level schools. This section considers the experience of case study schools in relation to this GEI.

Table 4.1: Total guidance resources in the case study schools

School	Size	Total Guidance
Hills Road	Small–Medium	11 hours
Beechwood Square	Medium	11 hours
Whitefield	Large	22 hours
Rosendale	Medium	22 hours
Willow Grove	Small	1.5 days/wk
Laurel Park	*Medium*	*44 hours*
Oakhill Way	Medium	11 hours
Maplewood	Medium–Large	32 hours
Lawton Way	Small	22 hours
Ashfield Park	*Medium*	*33 hours*
Seaview	Medium–Large	22 hours
Chestnut Drive	Large	19 hours
Riverbank	Medium–Large	22 hours
Greenwood	Large	22 hours
Cherryfield View	Medium	18 hours

Note: Italic type indicates GEI Schools

4.4.1 Awareness of GEI

Two of the 15 case study schools participated in the GEI. Of the remaining schools, just two applied and 11 did not apply to participate in the programme. The majority of the schools who did not apply for the Initiative had either very limited or no awareness of the programme and those who had some awareness felt they had little information on it. There were clear issues over awareness of the programme in the first place and understanding of it in the second. Many school Principals commented "I wouldn't be keenly aware of it" (Principal, Willow Grove) and "We didn't know about it on time" (Guidance Counsellor, Hills Road).

A number of schools felt they were ineligible because it was targeted at disadvantaged schools.

> No, [we can't avail of it] because we didn't consider we were disadvantaged. I considered it but having looked at the criteria surrounding it, it wasn't for us. (Principal, Oakhill Way).

Others felt certain types of schools were more likely to be accepted into the Initiative and maintained that "very few secondary schools got it" (Principal, Beechwood Square). One school didn't apply because they felt that they had been successful in their applications for other funding and had received good support from the Department.

> [We have] applied for so many other things here . . . we've had the LCA and the LCVP . . . we've had language hours . . . we've had the [*amount of funding*] Stay in School Initiative as well. I think the school would actually think seriously about what they're applying for and that they wouldn't be looking for everything that comes around. (Guidance Counsellor, Lawton Way).

Another felt that, while they had heard "bits and pieces" about the Initiative, since they had not been successful in their previous requests for additional guidance resources, there was little point in applying. Finally, one of the Guidance Counsellors suggested that the Principal's failure to apply for the GEI emanated from an insufficient appreciation of the work of the Guidance Counsellor.

4.4.2 Experience of GEI

As mentioned, two of the case study schools received extra funding under the GEI. One of the schools received a full-time (22 hours) guidance allocation while the other received a part-time (11 hours) allocation. In addition to these GEI resources and the basic allocation from the Department of Education and Science, both of these schools added an additional 11 hours from their teacher allocations to the guidance area. As noted above, a total of five of the case study schools added additional school resources to guidance above and beyond the standard departmental allocation. Thus the two GEI case study schools had significant guidance resources: the first, a medium sized school, had two full-time Guidance Counsellors and the second, again of medium size, had one full-time and one part-time Guidance Counsellor. According to the quota system of allocation from the Department of Education and Science, both schools would have received a part-time allocation had their guidance resources been based solely on that allocation.

The guidance experiences in these two GEI case study schools will be discussed under two areas: the use of (the additional) guidance resources and the perceived impact of the additional resources from the GEI.

4.4.3 Use of guidance resources

The two schools adopted different models for the use of the additional guidance resources. One used the additional funds to focus attention on a previously neglected group of students, namely junior cycle students (Ashfield Park). The other school separated the guidance role into two distinct positions: career guidance adviser and counsellor (Laurel Park).

Additional resources received through the GEI in Laurel Park allowed the Guidance Counselling role to be distributed across two key personnel: the Career Guidance Counsellor, focusing on academic and career guidance, and the Counsellor, concerned with personal and social support for students. The establishment of two separate guidance roles meant that there were effectively two people working in the area of counselling as the school also had a Chaplain.

The assignment of one Guidance Counsellor to the junior cycle and the other to senior cycle was seen as an important addition to the guidance services in Ashfield Park. Students are now exposed to career guidance from first year onwards.

> I met the first years on a one to one basis and checked in on how they were doing, settling in, [became aware of] any problems that were arising. I initiated a career programme, a careers investigation where I exposed them to options outside their own immediate environment. At the end of first year I worked with them towards subject choices bearing in mind the implications of the subject choices for later on in senior cycle and more importantly for careers opportunities post Leaving Cert. (Guidance Counsellor, Ashfield Park).

4.4.4 Impact of GEI: Laurel Park

Key personnel in both schools emphasised the extremely positive impact the GEI has had on their school. The separation of career and counselling roles in Laurel Park was seen as a major strength. It allowed one Guidance Counsellor to focus solely on career guidance.

> It's given him much more freedom in terms of developing more career related work with the students because in the past what would be expected of a Guidance Counsellor in terms of the sheer needs of our students really was impossible. (Guidance Counsellor, Laurel Park).

It has also enabled the provision of career guidance to fifth year and second year groups which wasn't possible prior to the GEI. In addition, the GEI played a central role in the provision of counselling for students in this school.

> . . . [the] traditional role of the Guidance Counsellor was probably very much guidance with a bit of counselling but the counselling element would have been very small . . . But the changes in society [have meant that] what we are meeting now is a lot of children with a lot of serious needs and we can provide that [support] to a certain degree here. I am not saying we are trying to do the job of social services but we can provide immediate qualified effective intervention until we get the other agencies on board. (Principal, Laurel Park).

4.4.5 Ashfield Park

The benefits of the GEI in the other case study school were seen in a number of areas. First, it targeted resources towards "disadvantaged" students. Second, it has functioned to raise awareness of guidance among students and, third, it allowed the introduction of chemistry (presumably through the promotion of the subject in career guidance fostering sufficient demand among students to introduce it) as well as promoting the sciences in general.

> Even just to raise the awareness of science because we didn't have chemistry up to last year. We had all physics. . . . I suppose to make the children aware that science when they go into fifth year can be interesting and it's not a difficult subject. They have a perception that it's hard. Now, I am happy with it. (Principal, Ashfield Park).

The guidance programme also placed emphasis on the link between industry and the area of science. Finally, it allowed greater contact with parents and a more proactive approach particularly regarding behavioural issues.

Chapters Two and Three also discussed variations in guidance and counselling services across GEI and non-GEI schools. Overall, schools participating in the GEI are more likely to have a more balanced range of guidance services across all year groups, have a greater range of career guidance and personal counselling activities and are more likely to have a guidance plan. Schools participating in the GEI, for example, were more satisfied with the support systems for students in their schools and were more positive about being able to address guidance issues within the allocated time.

4.5 ROLE OF THE GUIDANCE COUNSELLOR

4.5.1 Overall role of Guidance Counsellor

Schools varied widely in the nature of the Guidance Counsellor's role; particularly in terms of the range of activities of the Guidance Counsellor and the balance of time spent on the main areas of career guidance, academic/educational guidance and personal/social support. Guidance Counsellors in nine of the case study schools indicated that they spent the majority of their time, and in some cases all of their time, on career guidance and academic guidance. Guidance Counsellors in the remaining six schools tended to take a more "dual role": distributing their time more evenly between career/academic guidance and personal/social support and counselling for students.

Schools which tended to focus solely or predominantly on careers did so for a number of reasons which are discussed below. Among the more "career-guidance focused" schools were the following:

> Careers at the moment, it tends to vary from the time of year. . . . There are a few other issues as well but definitely I would put 75 per cent careers. (Guidance Counsellor, Hills Road).

> I would be very much [working on] the careers rather than the counselling side. (Guidance Counsellor, Maplewood).

> My role would be mainly careers . . . I generally don't get involved
> in the students' problems at all. . . . I really would not be able to give
> over time in any case to do much counselling. (Guidance Counsellor,
> Chestnut Drive).

The Guidance Counsellor in Riverbank highlighted the importance of
ensuring that each student gets "proper career information", so that students "would be able to face the Leaving Cert, CAO and changing to
third level". Similarly, the Guidance Counsellor in Greenwood noted that
"the emphasis would be very much on making sure that they all would
be aware of what is going on where, that they're well briefed, that they
can present themselves, that application forms are looked after care-
fully". However, this Guidance Counsellor did express concern that "the
counselling area, which I have a lot of interest in, sort of gets pushed
down very much because a lot of students want to deal with what they
want to do".

While a career focus was evident in the majority of schools, some
schools adopted a more holistic or dual role, encompassing academic/
career guidance and personal/social counselling:

> Our Guidance Counsellor would spend half her time doing counsel-
> ling and half time doing career guidance. (Principal, Whitefield).

> Initially [I concentrate on the] Leaving Cert to try and get them to
> focus on the type of career they want to pursue. [To] get them ready
> for CAO. First years, it's important to meet with them to see how
> they have coped with the transition from primary to secondary. And
> at the moment it's third years, to try and get them to decide on sub-
> jects for next year, that is all subject based. Then the counselling side
> is huge. (Guidance Counsellor, Rosendale).

4.5.2 Schools where Guidance Counsellor has career guidance focus

Schools tended to focus their activities on career guidance and preparation for three main reasons: the preference and definition adopted by the
Guidance Counsellor or school management, an attempt to meet the demands of parents and a need to prioritise focus in a context of limited resources. In many schools, the Guidance Counsellor defined their role as
one principally concerned with career guidance. They felt that their train-

ing and guidance function was one of career preparation and advice and carried out their activities accordingly. In some schools, the Guidance Counsellor felt that there was an expectation from parents that their child would receive comprehensive career/college preparation and they felt obliged to concentrate their efforts on such preparation for that reason.

In a number of schools, the predominant focus on careers arose due to a perceived lack of funding and time for guidance activities and the need to prioritise the college preparation of students within this context of limited resources. It was recognised that a greater focus on personal/social support for students was very desirable but was just not possible within the current allocation of funding.

A number of schools employed the services of trained psychotherapists to provide counselling and support for students, allowing the Guidance Counsellor to focus on career and academic areas.

> . . . as part of the school completion programme we are in a position to hire a counsellor and we have been doing that for some students who badly need it. (Principal, Rosendale).

> . . . having the Pathways psychologist on the premises two or three days a week is tremendous. Now that's mainly . . . with first years and second years. (Principal, Lawton Way).

Others saw local counselling services as the main source of (expert) counselling, while school-based Guidance Counsellors ensure career and academic guidance for students.

> That is where they would see the, the [name of area] services there [personal support/ counselling]. It's not ideal at all, there are occasions when you would really want somebody in house with the skills. There is lots of good will, very generous teachers, very generous Year Heads but sometimes when you meet aggression or withdrawal or just the depth to the problem that you just can't do it without referring them. (Guidance Counsellor, Chestnut Drive).

One Principal questioned the emphasis placed on career guidance across many schools, arguing that the process of selecting and applying for courses/colleges does not require the amount of "expertise" and emphasis that has developed.

> . . . the career thing is pumped up to be much, to be too important al-
> together, way beyond what it should be given in terms of importance
> or big deal, really. The CAO and all this muck, big industry around
> that, I mean kids go to college, Jesus everyone goes to college, they
> pick up subjects, it isn't a science, there's an industry built up around
> it and there's a whole new science of people who spend their whole
> life on the circuit, talking about admissions policies. (Principal,
> Seaview).

Where schools did place a heavy focus on the "career" element of the
Guidance Counsellor's role, such career guidance tended to be narrowly
framed in terms of college preparation and CAO applications. There appeared to be relatively little focus on career/job preparation more generally, except as part of the Vocational Preparation and Guidance component of the LCA programme, and non-third level options such as PLCs
or FÁS training courses were relatively neglected. Chapter Five considers students' views on this issue and draws out these imbalances in guidance focus and the implications for students and their choices.

4.5.3 Dual role

As noted earlier, one of the GEI schools (Laurel Park) used the additional resources received under the Initiative to allocate a Guidance
Counsellor solely to the area of counselling, functioning alongside a
Guidance Counsellor working in the area of career and academic guidance. While the first Guidance Counsellor "tends to concentrate very
much on career end, so he would be involved very much with subject
choice, taking students to visit various colleges, industries, very involved
with the Access programme with [name of university]"; the second
Guidance Counsellor describes her role as one which has "evolved more
into counselling full time", usually on a one-to-one basis. She also notes
spending a considerable amount of time liaising with child and adoles-
cent psychiatry, GPs and the Health Board.

A Guidance Counsellor in Oakhill Way noted that the increasing
availability of computer/internet resources around careers has allowed
her greater time and the opportunity to shift attention towards counselling.

A major concern in a large number of schools was a perception of rising need and demand for counselling, in the context of wider societal changes.

> Counselling is becoming increasingly more in demand in the last couple of years. We have a lot of children in need . . . they are referred to me, and if possible I would see them on a weekly basis until they feel they can go back into the class. (Guidance Counsellor, Ashfield Park).

However, some questioned the role of schools in the area of personal/social support and counselling for students and held that such a role should not be the concern of the Guidance Counsellor.

> . . . the counselling end, which I feel is a growing need within our school and other schools. It's challenging, the needs of society are changing and schools are not equipped to deal with many of the problems that manifest themselves here. (Principal, Riverbank).

Further, others questioned the extent to which schools should play a role more generally in this area (an issue which is discussed further in Chapter Six).

4.5.4 Other activities: Subject choice

Arrangements for advising students on subject choice varied from highly structured set class times for subject choice guidance to more ad hoc arrangements whereby students receive guidance regarding their subject choices at "free" times or by request of the student. Correspondingly, schools varied in the role the Guidance Counsellor played in the process of subject choice.

Schools adopting more structured subject guidance often involved parents in the process, particularly for decisions on junior cycle subject selection, and tended to place the Guidance Counsellor as central to the process of subject choice.

> . . . we would have a meeting of all the parents of the new first years coming in and the career guidance person would be there, among a lot of other teachers on the night to talk to the parents about their choice of subjects at first year and kind of give them a little birds eye

view of where these subjects will lead to in the future. (Principal, Greenwood).

Key personnel in subject choice advice

Two of the schools assigned the role of subject or academic guidance to other staff members. In one case, the Principal adopted the role, while in the other, the Tutors were seen as best placed to offer such advice.

> Well I would be there as advisory to the class teacher and to students if they need it, if a teacher asked me to go into a class to talk about subject choices I would go in, but by virtue of the fact that we have Year Head and Class Tutors who know the students very, very well, they would be more familiar with the educational background and educational strengths than I would be. (Guidance Counsellor, Lawton Way).

In other schools, there was more of a teamwork approach to subject guidance with a range of personnel playing a role in subject advice.

> . . . in the next week or two all third years who are going on to stay at school next year will be got [brought] together and the year head will talk to them about subjects and [name of Guidance Counsellor] will talk to them about careers. (Principal, Chestnut Drive).

Timing of junior cycle subject choice

The timing of subject choice for junior cycle students clearly plays a role in the scope and need for advice on subject choice. A number of schools offered taster programmes which allowed students to try out subjects for a period of time before selecting their subjects for the Junior Certificate.

However, in other schools, inflexibility in the timing of subject choice for junior cycle gave little scope for advice.

> [There is] no advice for first years . . . at the start of first year they are told the subjects that are on offer and then they select on the basis of that information. . . . That has to be done from day one of first year. (Guidance Counsellor, Oakhill Way).

Senior cycle subject and programme choice

Many of the Guidance Counsellors considered advising third and fourth year/TY students on senior cycle subject and programme choices as particularly important to their role. There was recognition of the importance of such choices for longer term educational and career opportunities.

> I don't deal with first years because they get a broad taste of everything but it becomes very important in fourth year, it's really the first step in career choice. Because if they choose the wrong subjects they can't get the career of their choice later. So that takes about a week between giving classes, seeing them individually, meeting with parents. (Guidance Counsellor, Maplewood).

> Well in third year . . . I'd deal with two things in particular, one is the way the Leaving Cert is organised . . . explain Transition Year, they have the Applied Leaving Cert, the Vocational Leaving and the standard Leaving Cert, what the implications are of taking any one of these and also what you actually will study [in these programmes]. (Guidance Counsellor, Greenwood).

4.5.5 Other activities: Work experience, ability testing, contact with parents

Guidance Counsellors did not generally take a central or co-ordinating role in students' work experience; often such a position was filled by programme co-ordinators, particularly for Transition Year and the Leaving Certificate Applied. One notable exception was Rosendale.

> I am in charge of the LCVP in fifth year. [Overseeing] their work experience, which has recently been completed. It's a lot of work, getting consent forms from parents, ringing employers and visiting them on work experience. Then I am also involved with LCA work experience. (Guidance Counsellor, Rosendale).

In almost all of the case study schools, students took part in ability testing prior to, or upon entry in, first year. Guidance Counsellors played a central role in such testing, sometimes with the assistance of learning support personnel.

4.5.6 Combining teaching and guidance roles

In six of the case study schools, Guidance Counsellors combined subject teaching with their guidance responsibilities. This was seen to create additional difficulties for a number of the Guidance Counsellors relating to the need to juggle two distinct roles and the two ways of relating to students, that is, in a teaching and disciplinary capacity and in a guidance and pastoral manner.

> One thing that is vitally important for Guidance Counsellors is that they are not seen as disciplinarians and that is one of the dilemmas for a career guidance teacher. If you want to be seen as a disciplinarian in one class . . . how are they going to come to you if they have a problem . . . that dilemma between class work and careers work. (Guidance Counsellor, Willow Grove).

4.5.7 Time with different year groups and Leaving Certificate Programmes

Departmental guidelines (2005) and documentation from the NCGE place a heavy emphasis on the provision of guidance and counselling services for all students across all year groups. However, as noted earlier, the nature of guidance services is largely discretionary in the sense that schools themselves decide on the way in which guidance resources are allocated within their school. The delivery of guidance services has, as a result, been heavily focused on senior cycle students, particularly sixth year students, with younger groups relatively neglected. As discussed later, this has serious implications for the extent to which students make informed subject and programme choices during junior cycle and as they progress into senior cycle. The career and educational constraints imposed by such uninformed choices are of concern. In addition, an imbalance in favour of sixth year students raises issues over whether younger students are fully aware of the implications of educational failure, non-attendance and early school leaving.

Senior cycle

In all of the case study schools, the Guidance Counsellor spent a considerable portion of their time with fifth and sixth year students.

The bulk of the work would be in what we call fourth and fifth year. Now other schools differ. Fourth years is the Leaving Certificate first year, and fifth year is the Leaving Certificate. (Principal, Chestnut Drive).

I do [work with] mainly the senior cycle people, I would have the LCA fifth and sixth years, I would have the fifth years for guidance. (Guidance Counsellor, Lawton Way).

Such senior cycle guidance was often offered through timetabled guidance classes and one-to-one appointments with students.

Transition Year

Schools offering the Transition Year option typically incorporated guidance classes within the programme.

With Transition Year I have a formal class as well of careers so I get them to research a particular career of their choice. And I also do work experience with that group. (Guidance Counsellor, Beechwood Square).

You get about six periods in fourth year and that is all about career investigation and getting them familiar with the information and what is available to them and make sure they use it and that they can come here at lunch time and discuss things. Also [I cover] subject choices for fifth and sixth year, that is really what the [TY careers] module is about. (Guidance Counsellor, Maplewood).

For those schools where the TY programme was optional, some time was devoted to third year students proceeding directly to the senior cycle: "I have a group of third years who go directly to fifth year and I have to do it [career guidance] with them as well". (Guidance Counsellor, Maplewood)

Career guidance within the Transition Year programme was seen as a worthwhile and beneficial experience, giving a good foundation for career decisions in fifth and sixth year. For many it was seen as the first step in the career process, giving crucial information and guidance for important subject and programme decisions for senior cycle:

Because if they [fourth years] choose the wrong subjects they can't get the career of their choice later. (Guidance Counsellor, Maplewood).

I find the transition year students have enough opportunities to experience these things. Yesterday they visited a university with me and they had a good lecture from one of the admissions officers in there about the different faculties. Then they were given a tour of the college and, you know, this can be helpful to them. (Guidance Counsellor, Willow Grove).

The study did not examine in great detail the nature of guidance activities for TY students. According to Transition Year Programme Guidelines (DES, 1993), however, the TY guidance programme should be designed to address the needs of all pupils so as to help them to:

- Assess and interpret information related to their abilities, interests, skills and achievements;

- Acquire competencies in educational and career exploration and planning;

- Develop knowledge of self and others and of the society in which they live;

- Develop realistic personal, social, educational and vocational goals.

Findings of a recent study (Smyth, Byrne and Hannan, 2004), however, illustrate quite a variation across schools in the level and nature of guidance in Transition Year and whether it is offered as a structured programme or on a more ad hoc basis.

Junior cycle

Few Guidance Counsellors devoted any significant amount of their guidance time to junior cycle students. Work by the NCGE (Audit of 1999-2000) and Chapters Two and Three further illustrate the lack of attention to junior cycle students. According to the NCGE (1999/2000), 25 per cent of schools reported that no Guidance Counsellor time was spent with junior cycle students. The smaller the school the more likely the Guidance Counsellor spent no time with junior cycle students. They also found some variation across school types: 35 per cent of vocational schools and community colleges, 21 per cent of secondary schools and 14 per cent of community and comprehensive schools reported that the Guidance Counsellor did not spend time with junior cycle students. There was little difference in provision between schools with a disadvantaged post and schools without a disadvantaged post.

Third years

Many of the schools did offer *some* subject and programme choice guidance to junior cycle students, usually in third year where the Transition Year programme was not available.

> . . . the process begins in third year when they choose subjects for fifth and sixth year. At the moment we are in the throws of subject choice and tonight I have all of the third year parents and students coming to a meeting. (Guidance Counsellor, Ashfield Park).

Some Guidance Counsellors also incorporate study and exam techniques into their guidance programme with third year students, which is seen as particularly useful in the context of the impending Junior Certificate examination.

> Then in third year [I would cover] study techniques and exam techniques and an introduction to career guidance. I find if they have an idea of what they would like to do it motivates them to think the Junior Cert is important. (Guidance Counsellor, Oakhill Way).

Often guidance activities with third year students revolved around some type of aptitude test, with the results of these tests guiding their subject choices for senior cycle.

> I do the DATS, I do the differential aptitude test in third year and I would give them the results and we would discuss subject choice with them. (Guidance Counsellor, Seaview).

First and second years

With the exception of Ashfield Park (where additional GEI resources were targeted at junior cycle guidance), most of the schools did not place a strong emphasis on career guidance for first and second year students.

Where Guidance Counsellors do indicate some contact with first and second year students, it is largely unstructured.

> I speak to first years about choosing, they have to select a few options going into second year, that would be on a random basis, I wouldn't have any formal contact with any junior classes in [the] school. (Guidance Counsellor, Beechwood Square).

The transition from primary school was an area of attention for Guidance Counsellors in a number of schools. The Guidance Counsellor's role also included assisting first year students in getting settled into the new school by providing them with necessary information.

> When they are in about three weeks I go to all first year classes and I take a settling-in class with them. What they like about it, the names of the teachers and their subjects and how they are settling in, the names of their classmates, an orientation towards the school. Then about ten days later I would have another appointment with the class group and I would go through study skills and discuss the difference between primary and secondary school. (Guidance Counsellor, Whitefield).

Several schools identified a need for greater, or at least some, guidance at junior cycle, but constraints on resources and time were seen to restrict such options. One of the schools expressed the following view, a view which was echoed in ten of the case study schools.

> Interviewer: What would be the main priorities for the future?
>
> Deputy Principal: That you would target the junior school, in career guidance. And that a programme would be put in place that a child would be aware from first year on that decisions are going to be made about her life even if she doesn't make them but she is aware of the consequences of subject choices. (Beechwood Square).

Some did, however, question the value of initiating career guidance at such a young age and argued that post-Junior Certificate was a more appropriate time to start thinking about and investigating careers.

> I remember over the years, way back . . . talking to first and second years about university and third level, it was all over their heads, they weren't interested. (Principal, Greenwood).

Yet others felt that concentrating all career choices and decision-making during sixth year placed excessive pressure on students.

> . . . the process of choice and the decision-making is shortened into sixth year, right. Instead of it being spread out over five years, and because they are so pressurised in sixth year anyway they might make a bad choice because their energies are diverted elsewhere. (Guidance Counsellor, Maplewood).

4.5.8 Leaving Certificate programmes

As discussed earlier, some schools offered Junior Certificate and TY students guidance regarding their choice of Leaving Certificate programmes. Such guidance often involved an open night with parents, as well as students, informing them about the programmes available in the school.

> . . . the way the Leaving Cert is organised . . . explain Transition Year, they have the Applied Leaving Cert, the Vocational Leaving and the standard Leaving Cert, what the implications are of taking any one of these and also what you actually will study. (Guidance Counsellor, Greenwood).

Leaving Certificate students usually differed in terms of the nature and level of guidance received according to the Leaving Certificate option they were undertaking, that is, the regular Leaving Certificate, the LCVP and the LCA.

A number of Guidance Counsellors worked on the career module for LCA and LCVP students.

> I would do a lot of work in LCVP, that takes up a huge amount of my time. Because we have 60 [students] doing LCVP in this school and the career investigation is specialised and only a careers person can do it, properly. Because nobody else would know where the various careers, where do you go to research this, so that is huge for me. . . . And I couldn't take 60 together; it has to be on a modular

basis. So I always have a group of fifth years in LCVP that I am seeing. (Guidance Counsellor, Maplewood).

But then as part of the LCA in fifth and sixth year the Guidance
Counsellor works with the reflective task part of LCA, so he's timetabled to work with LCA, he's also timetabled to work with fifth
year, the other fifth year group. We sometimes have LCVP as well,
the vocational programme. (Principal, Lawton Way).

In addition, the Guidance Counsellor in Beechwood Square also assisted
the LCA students, with the aim of trying to expand their horizons and
inform them of the range of post-school options open to them.

I work with LCA students, [year] one and two, I have one period per
week for it and again it's on research[ing] career[s], advising them
on work placements and helping them with CVs, interview skills and
try[ing] to open up their minds to possibilities that are out there. I
think that group are very closed and [have] only one or two careers
in mind. (Guidance Counsellor, Beechwood Square).

Reflecting the structure, content and nature/methodologies of the LCVP
and LCA programmes, a number of key school personnel identified a
difference in the level of preparation of students for life beyond school.
Most notably, staff commented on the greater labour market "readiness"
of LCVP and, particularly, LCA students following their participation in
the programme compared to students following the established Leaving
Certificate.

The LCA prepares them a bit better for work, they do work experience one day a week . . . they would be better prepared for life afterwards. (Deputy Principal, Seaview).

The LCA group is far more prepared for the interview situation, interacting with adults, knowledge of the work place. They would be
interacting with managerial people within the work place, they
would definitely be far better prepared, that would be very much part
of the process they go through as part of the course. (Principal, Laurel Park).

The findings are largely in line with departmental guidelines on the role of the Guidance Counsellor in the LCVP and LCA programmes, guidelines that make explicit the role a Guidance Counsellor might play.

> In addition to the Co-ordinator, the LCVP team will be drawn from teachers of the Link Modules, specialist teachers from the Vocational Subject Groupings, the Guidance Counsellor and teacher/s providing ICT access. (LCVP Guidelines DES, 1999).

Within the LCA, the Vocational Preparation and Guidance component (VPG) is a major part of the programme and one which the guidelines explicitly state as "the only module that requires delivery by a qualified Guidance Counsellor" (DES, 2000) The aims of the module include a focus on awareness of interests, skills and personality, access to and the use of information, developing a career action plan and self-review.

However, there is an issue over whether guidance counselling provision in VPG is adequate across schools and whether in fact there is any timetabled provision. A recent evaluation of the LCA (2001) noted that the time allocated by schools for VPG was not always as recommended, with the time allocation less than the minimum recommended in a number of instances (p. 2). This report recommended that the Guidance Counsellor should be timetabled for one period a week in Year One and be available to Year Two students individually as required.

4.6 ACCESS TO GUIDANCE

Schools varied in whether they allocated timetabled classes to (predominantly senior cycle) students or followed an appointment system whereby students are allocated an appointment, or encouraged to make an appointment, to see the Guidance Counsellor. In many schools, a combination of the two approaches was used.

Table 4.2: Nature of access to guidance

School	Appointments or Classroom Based
Hills Road	Classes
Beechwood Square	Mixed
Whitefield	Mixed
Rosendale	18 classes/wk, remainder appointments
Willow Grove	Nearly all classes
Laurel Park	Some classes, much time on appointments
Oakhill Way	Half and half
Maplewood	4-5 hrs in class, 17 in office – admin, meetings and appointments
Lawton Way	Mixed
Ashfield Park	Classes
Seaview	Mixed
Chestnut Drive	Appointments
Riverbank	Mixed
Greenwood	Mixed
Cherryfield View	Appointments

Even where schools operate an appointment system for guidance access, schools varied in the nature of appointments - some operate on a voluntary appointment system while others have "compulsory" appointments.

> . . . it's compulsory, I issue appointments to them. In fact I issued three appointments to all fifth years this year. And beyond that then I leave it open for them. (Guidance Counsellor, Cherryfield View).

Most Guidance Counsellors adopted a traditional didactic teaching methodology in their classes. In terms of more innovative methodologies such as group-work, just one Chaplain adopted a small-group set-up.

> I took them [first years] in a small group and individually. . . . I also meet with fourth and fifth years. [and also second and third years] I would meet them in groups. [There were] maybe eight or ten in a group. (Chaplain, Riverbank).

However, this Chaplain did allude to the difficulties of such group-work, as some students were too self-conscious to talk about personal issues in front of other students.

> Interviewer: How does that work [groupwork], does it work as well as individual meetings?
>
> Chaplain: No, it doesn't. Guys wouldn't be as free to talk, they are more self-conscious. They won't talk about personal things. (River-bank).

Others argued that a full-class situation is ineffective and smaller group work would be preferable.

> I also wonder about the value, especially [if] you're talking about re-lationships and friendships and even the issue of self confidence and self awareness and all of that, talking to that same group of thirty I just think the size of classes, I think quite honestly it's a bit of a joke . . . the groups need to be smaller, ten or twelve to do any sort of ef-fective work. (Chaplain, Greenwood).

The need for more one-to-one work was seen to be a particularly impor-tant issue at senior cycle, but again time and resource constraints were seen to hinder the provision of such a guidance service. Other difficulties in addressing guidance and counselling issues in a whole-class setting surrounded discipline and interest levels in class groups.

> It's fairly difficult if you don't teach a class you don't have them every day. And to go into a class, especially a big class, it's difficult for the career guidance teacher. It's sometimes very difficult. Chil-dren being what they are they only see this lady once a week and some of them don't have a huge interest in what she would be say-ing, it wouldn't apply to them. (Deputy Principal, Chestnut Drive).

However, some did see benefits in having timetabled classes, particularly in ensuring contact with every student.

> Interviewer: What would you see as the main strengths of the guid-ance and counselling service in this school?
>
> Guidance Counsellor: The fact it's timetabled. Not everybody wants that. But it reduces considerably the one to one access because they

> are going to see me once a week every week and I can generate and
> hand out and collect and whatever. (Whitefield).

In sum, Guidance Counsellors face a dilemma in deciding the nature of
guidance contact with their students. While timetabled classes ensure
contact with all students and a certain uniformity in content, they do create difficulties in maintaining interest levels and ensuring relevance to all
students. On the other hand, one-to-one appointments allowed guidance
meetings to be tailored to individual need, but resource constraints limit
the number of such contacts and the availability of the Guidance Counsellor for such appointments.

4.7 LINKS WITH THE CURRICULUM

For many of the Guidance Counsellors and other staff involved in a pastoral capacity in their school, pastoral care is seen as complemented by
the introduction of new curricular programmes, most notably SPHE (Social, Personal and Health Education) and RSE (Relationships and Sexu-
ality Education Programme).

For a number of staff, the introduction of SPHE is seen as a valuable
addition to the curriculum, in giving a broader definition of student development and attainment.

> Interviewer: Would you think that these new curricular areas like the
> SPHE are a positive move?
>
> Guidance Counsellor: Absolutely, they are critical, they are marvel-
> lous and in fact I was thinking . . . if I could do in-service myself to
> get to know what is there and to be up-to-date. (Riverbank).

However, some did question the methodology, in particular the value of
teaching and discussing sensitive and personal issues in a whole class
setting. It would seem such classes are most beneficial in raising awareness and understanding of social and personal issues rather than actually
dealing with individual student concerns.

Others expressed concern at the exam-focused nature of the system
and the difficulties in promoting non-exam curricular areas, such as
SPHE and CSPE, to parents and students. The process of shifting focus
beyond the examinations towards more general social, personal and edu-

cational development is one that requires a change in mindset among students and their parents and is likely to take some time to achieve.

> . . . second-level [education] is so much geared towards exams. . . . You would love to give more time to do subjects like SPHE and CSPE and maybe RE, places where kids can discuss and talk and explore. But if you ask the teachers well will you give up a maths class, no they won't. Ask parents would you prefer SPHE or an extra class of maths they will say maths. The exam system certainly has a great stranglehold on what you can do. (Principal, Rosendale).

Overall a number of schools questioned the level of co-ordination between guidance, pastoral care and curricular programmes such as SPHE and RE. One or more of these areas was seen to be duplicating efforts in another area.

> But also the SPHE course covers, or we cover a lot of what our religion programme would have covered. If a school isn't taking up on religion as an exam course, and are following the old course, the SPHE is just re-hashing the same thing. . . . As well as that the CSPE programme . . . overlaps with other programmes, religion and basic SPHE. . . . So the three programmes [are] totally overlapping. And there seems to be no uniformity or continuity in organisation. (Deputy Principal, Cherryfield View).

The need for greater co-ordination and more of a team-based approach to guidance and support issues was also emphasised in a number of schools.

> It needs to be seen as part of the pastoral care, the SPHE, and guidance, as a team facility that would be in the school rather than an individual trying to provide the service. . . . Definitely [there needs to be] more [of] a team effort. (Principal, Beechwood Square).

These issues are further addressed in Chapter Six; in particular, the notion of a whole school approach to guidance and student support and the extent of co-ordination among staff are discussed.

4.8 LINKS WITH PARENTS

In many schools, the work of the Guidance Counsellor also involves working with parents; some relating to talks or information nights on various educational and social topics while others are involved in more specific issues such as parenting skills or literacy programmes. Some of this work is in conjunction with the work of the Home School Community Liaison officer (HSCL), while other Guidance Counsellors, in the absence of such a key support, took on a role with parents directly.

Much of the work with parents relates to the provision of information and advice around subjects and subject level options, programme choice and third level options. In many cases, parents were made aware of the range of choices on offer, the nature and content of the different subjects and programmes and the implications of different choices. Often parents were unaware of the choices on offer and the content of newer curricular programmes such as the LCA or more recently introduced subjects, so contact with, and information received from, the Guidance Counsellor is of great importance to many parents.

> She [the Guidance Counsellor] would talk to the parents, we have the subject option night tonight where we go through the LCA, LCVP and explain what those programmes mean to the parents. The child will be with them, which is a huge departure for us. We will have the results of the last three years. Before the child would have made decisions and the parents weren't aware of them. But now we talk about it and then she [the Guidance Counsellor] sets up meetings for them. (Principal, Ashfield Park).

> I see part of my role, especially in third year as informing parents or trying to educate them to some extent, maybe educate is not the right word but at least keep them briefed as to what is available [post-school], irrespective of the ability of a child. (Guidance Counsellor, Greenwood).

A number of schools had brought in "expert" speakers on specific topics, such as drugs, alcohol or suicide, which parents were invited to attend. While schools varied widely in the extent to which they ran such information evenings, they did seem an important way of raising awareness and understanding among parents and students alike of important social issues.

> The school actually brings in people to talk about drugs and drink to the school. And they also offer this to parents to attend these talks in the evening. (Guidance Counsellor, Willow Grove).

In a number of schools, the parents' council plays a role in organising events for parents and students. In some cases, the parents' council had taken on the role of organising a careers night, bringing in former students to talk about their experiences of their chosen career.

> They [the Parents' Council] organised a careers night for our sixth years where they drew on past pupils, they contacted past pupils to come back to the school to speak about their careers. (Deputy Principal, Beechwood Square).

As mentioned, many Guidance Counsellors saw their role as working with parents as well as with students. For some, their work with parents was seen to be an important means of helping students. Some of the work involved literacy programmes for parents.

> I would have been responsible for getting people [parents] to go and take part in literacy programmes, [they were] not able to read and write themselves and through my relationship with them they have dealt with that. I would always have worked on the premise that if you can help the parents you are helping the children. (Guidance Counsellor, Ashfield Park).

Parenting skills was also covered, as were issues of personal development, while parents' groups were also set up in a number of schools.

A number of school personnel and Guidance Counsellors did express concerns over the time available and the role of the school and teachers in terms of working with parents.

> . . . teachers understandably see themselves as teaching in the classroom so some people do have a problem with where does it start and finish. How much responsibility do I have to take, do I have to take this into account or, you know. A lot of people feel we don't have training for this [working with parents]. (Deputy Principal, Hills Road).

Some Guidance Counsellors indicated that, above and beyond meeting parents at parent-teacher meetings, they did not see their role as working with parents. However, such Guidance Counsellors were very much in a minority, and the over-whelming response was for Guidance Counsellors to consider their role as intricately connected with parents spanning a range of educational, personal and social domains. Such a role with parents seems greatly important and one that should be promoted, particularly in the context of students relying heavily on their parents in making educational and career choices. As discussed in Chapter Five, school leavers indicate that their parents are the primary source of advice on post-school decisions. Clearly parents need to be incorporated into the process of educational and career selection, choices relating to subject and programme options and post-school educational and career selection.

4.9 WRITTEN GUIDANCE PLAN

Just three of the 15 case study schools (Hills Road, Oakhill Way and Seaview) had a separate written guidance plan in place, while three further schools indicated that the guidance area was incorporated into their school plan (Maplewood, Lawton Way and Greenwood).

Guidance Counsellors in a number of schools seemed unsure as to the existence of a guidance plan and in one school the two Guidance Counsellors held differing views as to whether the school had completed a written guidance plan.

These figures are further supported by the NCGE (1999/2000) Audit of Schools illustrating that only 14 per cent of schools had a Whole School Development Plan, and of these 75 per cent made reference to guidance. Of the 86 per cent of schools that did not have a Whole School Development Plan, only 25 per cent had a written school guidance programme.

These findings are contrary to Department of Education and Science Guidelines (2005) whereby "each school is required to develop and implement, as a part of its overall plan, a comprehensive guidance plan, taking into account the needs of students, available resources and contextual factors".

Although only three schools had put a separate written guidance plan in place, a large number placed great emphasis on the importance of having a guidance plan and saw it as a key priority for the future.

> Interviewer: What would you see as the main priorities for the future?
>
> Guidance Counsellor: Planning is one of the essential elements. (Ashfield Park).

A number saw the absence of a guidance plan as a reflection of the standing of guidance in the school and the priority given to guidance. As one Guidance Counsellor commented:

> Yes, I think that it should be more of a whole school effort plan. Rather than almost [on] an ad-hoc basis. There is no big policy surrounding the guidance area in [the] school, I feel maybe it could be an area for growth in our school. (Beechwood Square).

Others alluded to a lack of time for planning generally and the increasingly onerous demands being placed on schools with regard to planning and the need to have policies in place in a wide range of areas.

> Sometimes I refer to the school planning and it's a little bit like trying to have your car serviced while travelling at seventy miles an hour on the motorway, because you're not allowed stop the school, you're actually supposed to do the service while everything is going on and that is very, very difficult, . . . I think we've got seventy or eighty [policies] now at the latest count, and every time I look there's another policy you're supposed to have and it just goes on and on and on. (Principal, Lawton Way).

4.10 SUMMARY AND DISCUSSION

Interviews with key personnel in the case study schools drew attention to the status of Guidance Counsellors in second-level schools and the extent to which they can be viewed as a separate professional group. There were issues over awareness of the role of the Guidance Counsellor in a number of schools. More generally, schools varied widely in the extent to which there was a whole school, or even team-based, approach to the provision of guidance and support services for students. Indeed few schools had developed a written school guidance plan, although many recognised the importance of undertaking such an exercise.

The issue of guidance resources was prominent in case study interviews. While there was little evidence of the underutilisation of guidance resources, as earlier work has suggested (NCGE, 2001), there was strong criticism of the resources currently devoted to guidance and the system of allocation of resources. However, schools varied widely in actual guidance personnel with several schools drawing on additional discretionary funds to meet guidance needs. In addition, two schools were participating in the GEI.

The lack of guidance resources has important implications for the nature and level of guidance provision in schools. Many felt the need to focus on the career guidance of senior cycle students, with relative neglect of career guidance for junior cycle students and relatively little attention being devoted to personal/social support for students in many schools. While recent curricular innovations such as SPHE were seen to have gone some way in offering such personal/social education for young people, there were criticisms over the allocation of staff to such subject areas and the level of co-ordination with the role of the Guidance Counsellor.

Overall, Guidance Counsellors expressed great difficulty in juggling teaching and guidance duties (a division of role which was particularly likely in smaller schools given the allocation of resources). Such Guidance Counsellors fulfilling teaching duties also expressed difficulty in being able to avail of in-service training.

Overall, participation in the GEI was found to have positive results. Guidance Counsellors in GEI schools were more likely to allocate time to junior cycle groups, they were more likely to fulfil a broader range of guidance duties and they expressed greater satisfaction with the nature and level of guidance and personal/social support services for their students.

Chapter Five

STUDENT PERSPECTIVES ON GUIDANCE PROVISION

5.1 INTRODUCTION

While literature in the area of guidance counselling services in Irish schools is sparse, there is a particular neglect of students' own experiences of guidance counselling. Research undertaken by the NCGE and IGC focuses exclusively on school Principals and Guidance Counsellors themselves, with little consideration of students' views on the nature of guidance and support they receive. This study places an important emphasis on students' experiences and attitudes, arguing that a comprehensive analysis of guidance counselling services in schools must consider the consumers of the service, that is, students themselves. The study draws on two main sources on information on students' views and experiences: the first is the Annual School Leavers' Survey giving crucial national data on the main sources of advice on the post-school choices of young people. The second source of information derives from focus groups with Junior and Leaving Certificate students in the 15 case study schools. Such focus groups discussed the timing and nature of advice on junior and senior cycle choices, students' satisfaction with advice received and their views on the personal and social support/counselling available to them in school.

5.2 SCHOOL LEAVERS' EXPERIENCE OF GUIDANCE AT SCHOOL

Evidence from the Annual School Leavers' Survey 2002[8] provides a useful complement to the information obtained through the focus groups with students in the case study schools (Sections 5.3 to 5.6). It allows an analysis of the main sources of advice on post-school choices according to the stage of leaving school and gender. It is based on a nationally representative sample of young people who left school during the 2000/01 academic year.

As shown in Table 5.1, school leavers report different sources of advice regarding their post school educational and labour market choices, with patterns of advice strongly related to educational attainment levels. Young people leaving school prior to Junior Certificate level are particularly unlikely to receive advice from school personnel, probably a reflection of the lack of focus within schools on junior cycle guidance, as well as the legal requirement to remain in school until the age of 16 years. Interestingly, such unqualified school leavers are also least likely to report receiving advice from external sources such as their parents, other family members or their friends.

Young people reporting that they received advice from their Guidance Counsellor or other teacher rises steadily according to the level of educational attainment: 40 per cent of Junior Certificate school leavers report receiving advice from their Guidance Counsellor, rising to 50 per cent among those leaving during senior cycle and 82 per cent among Leaving Certificate holders. However, this leaves 18 per cent of young people leaving school following the Leaving Certificate exam not receiving advice on their options from a Guidance Counsellor. One-quarter of young people leaving having completed the LCA or LCVP failed to report having received advice from their Guidance Counsellor.

In terms of the most helpful source of advice on post-school decisions, those leaving school prior to Leaving Certificate are more likely to report advice from their parents while those who remain in school to sit the Leaving Certificate are more likely to report their Guidance Counsel-

---

[8] A description of the Annual School Leavers' Survey is included in Chapter One, Methodology.

lor as a source of advice (Table 5.2). It is also worth noting that LCA students are more likely to report advice from a teacher (15 per cent) than students following the established Leaving Certificate programme (6 per cent), the latter being more likely to report advice from the Guidance Counsellor as being most helpful. This raises questions over the key school personnel allocated guidance duties with LCVP and, particularly, LCA students, particularly since Departmental guidelines require that a qualified Guidance Counsellor delivers the VPG module of the LCA programme. However, it may well be that programme co-ordinators are playing a more important "guidance" role with LCA and LVCP students and the operation of work experience as part of these programmes may also be fulfilling an important guidance role, which would not be available to students following the established Leaving Certificate programme.

Table 5.3 indicates some important gender differences in career advice during second-level education. Regardless of educational attainment, young males are more reliant on the advice of their parents while females are more likely to consider within-school advice, particularly advice from their Guidance Counsellor, as most helpful in making career decisions. Unfortunately it is not possible to identify whether such gender patterns are related to male and female students' openness to guidance in school or the extent to which males and females are actually offered such advice.

In sum, the survey highlights the important role of parents in the educational and labour market choices of young people. Regardless of educational attainment upon leaving school, parents represent a key source of advice on post-school choices. Such advice is particularly important among those leaving school prior to Leaving Certificate standard, suggesting the important role for policy in conveying career guidance information to parents, particularly for those at risk of early school leaving. If students are to be made aware of the choices they can make and the implications of choices such as early school leaving, it seems vital that parents are included in attempts to do so. Such parental inclusion in career guidance and promoting awareness and understanding of educational choices seems particularly important for males at risk of early leaving.

Table 5.1: Sources of advice on post-school choices by stage left school, SLS 2002

% Receiving advice re post-school decisions from the following:	Stage Left School					
	No Quals (%)	*Junior Cert (%)*	*Studying senior cycle (%)*	*LC Estab. (%)*	*LCA (%)*	*LCVP (%)*
Guidance Counsellor	21.2	40.0	50.4	81.6	75.1	74.7
Other teacher	19.3	27.0	38.7	40.3	42.8	38.0
Parent(s)	57.5	73.0	75.8	75.5	75.5	69.8
Other family member	18.5	19.9	23.8	26.6	18.6	23.9
Friend(s)	12.1	18.3	28.0	26.5	24.2	23.2
Other	6.2	3.2	7.6	8.1	8.1	5.2

Table 5.2: Who was most helpful in deciding what to do after school, SLS 2002

Most helpful source of advice re post-school decisions	Stage Left School					
	No Quals (%)	*Junior Cert (%)*	*Studying senior cycle (%)*	*LC Estab. (%).*	*LCA (%)*	*LCVP (%)*
Guidance Counsellor	12.3	16.7	23.7	45.1	38.0	40.5
Other teacher	6.5	6.3	9.2	5.9	14.6	7.8
Parent(s)	70.5	66.1	50.6	36.7	36.4	36.1
Other family member	2.9	5.6	6.0	4.3	3.0	9.6
Friend(s)	3.6	3.5	8.0	4.4	4.5	3.2
Other	4.3	1.7	2.5	3.7	3.5	2.8

Table 5.3: Gender variations in who was most helpful, SLS 2002

Most helpful source of advice re post-school decisions	Males				Females			
	No Quals (%)	*JC (%)*	*LC Any (%)*	*All (%)*	*No Quals (%)*	*JC (%)*	*LC Any (%)*	*All (%)*
Guidance Counsellor	9.9	16.3	40.9	36.1	15.2	25.9	46.8	44.4
Other teacher	4.9	6.2	5.7	5.8	8.5	8.2	7.6	7.6
Parent(s)	75.4	61.9	41.2	45.4	64.4	54.6	32.3	34.8
Other family member	1.2	6.6	5.0	5.2	5.0	4.4	5.2	5.2
Friend(s)	3.7	7.8	4.2	4.7	3.5	3.7	4.1	4.1
Other	4.9	1.3	3.0	2.8	3.5	3.2	4.0	3.9

5.3 CASE STUDY ANALYSIS: PROVISION AT JUNIOR CYCLE

Group interviews were carried out with Junior Certificate students in seven of the case-study schools. Among other issues, these interviews explored the advice students had received on making their junior cycle subject choices. The case-study schools varied in the extent of contact junior cycle students had with the Guidance Counsellor. In two of the seven schools, students had had no contact with the Guidance Counsellor and reported that they had received no formal advice on subject choice. In two of the schools, students had had some contact with the Guidance Counsellor in first year either in the form of a talk on the available options or in terms of aptitude tests followed by feedback. In the remaining three schools, the groups had had contact with the Guidance Counsellor in relation to their senior cycle subject choices but did not report any specific guidance at an earlier stage.

In four of the schools, students emphasised that they would have liked more advice on subject choices at an early stage focusing, for example, on the implications of taking different subjects. In contrast, two of the groups did not feel there was a great necessity for such advice at junior cycle level. In one school, students were divided about whether they would have liked more help with subject choices in first year. Having a taster programme was seen as helpful in two of the schools. However, students in one of these schools stressed they would have liked a longer taster programme:

> It would have been better if you had a year or something like that and just look at the different subjects.
>
> Interviewer: You'd like more time to look at the different options?
>
> Yeah because now at this stage in third year you start to wonder did you make the right decisions in some areas like science and business studies. (Junior Cert students, Greenwood).

Senior cycle students were also asked about their experiences of guidance at the junior cycle level. Students' comments tended to focus on the process whereby they made their choice of subjects for senior cycle. However, some students also referred to their choice of Junior Certificate subjects. In the latter case, students tended to report that they would have liked more guidance on their choice of subjects in first year in particular or throughout the course of junior cycle in general. Some students also mentioned that a taster programme would have helped them to choose their subjects.

In terms of senior cycle choices, schools differed in the amount of guidance given to students. Only one of the schools (Riverbank) had a highly structured approach with students being given classes in third year to help with their subject choices. In addition, students in three of the case-study schools reported that they had taken aptitude tests in third (or fourth) year to inform their choices and were given advice from the Guidance Counsellor on the basis of their test results:

> We did an aptitude test as well in fourth year and that is what we based it [our choice] on.
>
> Interviewer: They gave you the feedback after you did the test?
>
> Yeah, that was to help us pick our subjects for fifth year, that is why we did it in fourth year.
>
> [They] had the results then for you, he showed us, when we choose what course we might want to do he told us well that will suit you or not from the aptitude tests. (LCE students, Laurel Park).

The most common approach was for students to be given a formal talk or other advice from the Guidance Counsellor on the different senior cycle options. In one of the schools, senior cycle subject choice was also seen as facilitated by having a taster approach in Transition Year:

> I think if you come from third year you have a bigger problem, like in fourth year you have more of an opportunity to find out what you are doing. (LCE students, Maplewood).

However, in three of the case-study schools, students reported that they were given little or no formal guidance in choosing their senior cycle subjects.

In the school where students had third year classes on subject choice (Riverbank), students appeared broadly satisfied with the advice they had been given. However, across the other case-study schools, students generally felt that they had been given too little guidance in choosing their senior cycle subjects:

> You are not aware in junior cycle what way to go, I think they should have a session with the third years when you are choosing subjects. It's too late when you get into sixth year. It's more beneficial to get it in third year than sixth year. (LCE/LCVP students, Rosendale).

> I think when we picked the subjects for fifth and sixth year, I don't think you are greatly informed. (LCE students, Whitefield).

First, many students reported that they did not have adequate information on the content of specific senior cycle subjects:

> Like I did physics first time round and from the Junior Cert it's so vague on physics and then you are just thrown straight into the deep end in fifth year. I had no idea, I hated it. That kinda ruined my whole fifth year and I had to repeat it again. So it was a waste of a year.
>
> Interviewer: Do you think if you had've got better advice?
>
> Yeah, if I had've known more about the subject I wouldn't have gone near it.

Yeah, it's really important to know what is on the course, on the syllabus because I chose chemistry and I only chose that because to begin with I wanted to do veterinary but I have changed now, but I actually didn't know what was on the chemistry course and it's totally different to what I imagined it to be. (LCE students, Beechwood Square).

I just wrote down whatever, history, I did history in third year, it's completely different in fifth year, there's loads of writing and I hate it now, I used to love it in third year. (LCE/LCVP students, Greenwood).

Some subjects like commerce, like it's all theory but you don't know that like in third year. (LCVP students, Whitefield).

Secondly, the implications of taking particular senior cycle subjects for access to third-level courses was also a concern among many students:

I wanted to do speech and language but then I needed a science to start with. I can't do that because I don't have any science, I only figured that out in sixth year so it was too late to do anything about it then like. Even if it was the middle of fifth year, I could have taken something up. (LCE students, Beechwood Square).

Because you don't know what you are picking. Like in third year you are not worried what college you are going to but the subjects you pick might be the wrong ones.

I don't know, it's kind of left up to yourself in third year and then you are stuck with the choices in subjects you made.

Yeah I wanted to do art so in second year I had to pick art or French so I picked art because I was better at art and I thought that is what I wanted to do but I have changed now and if I wanted to go to college I would need French more, you need a language for college. (LCE students, Ashfield Park).

I know people who dropped French but then found out they needed it.

A lot of people did that this year.

When you don't know.

Interviewer: There was nobody telling them?

For the last two years French wasn't optional. They made an option of it and people who didn't like it dropped it but now they need it. (LCVP students, Whitefield).

People are finding out now they don't have the subjects. (LCE students, Maplewood).

Some students felt they had been given inaccurate information about third-level course requirements:

When I went in to see her [Guidance Counsellor], the one time I ever went to see her and I went in and I said I wanted to do engineering and she said to have a language, so I dropped Physics and took up French but now I don't have the science subject so I am screwballed for engineering. (LCVP students, Whitefield).

You think there should be more from the Guidance Counsellor but when I was in third year making my choices at the time I wanted to do home economics and she told me all the wrong subjects. She told me to do chemistry and then I found out you don't need that, "who told you that?", like she did. (LCE students, Ashfield Park).

One group of students also stressed that it was difficult to choose subjects before knowing how they had performed in their Junior Certificate exam:

We did things in third year but it was too early, you hadn't even done your Junior Cert, you had to pick them [subjects] after Christmas in third year. You don't know what you are good at. (LCVP students, Whitefield).

Another group felt that the decision about subject choice was made at too early a stage:

You can't be deciding what you're going to do when you're fifteen, you're not going to know exactly what you want to do in college when you're only fifteen and you have to pick subjects then. (LCE students, Seaview).

While discussions with students mainly focused on their choice of senior cycle subjects, the choice of different Leaving Certificate programmes was also mentioned by students. Two groups of students taking the Leaving Certificate Applied programme felt that they had not been given adequate guidance on the choice of senior cycle programmes, in particular on the options in terms of courses and careers which would be open to them afterwards. Another LCA group felt they should have been given such information at an earlier stage.

Overall, only two groups of students interviewed felt that the appropriate emphasis for guidance provision was on senior rather than junior cycle. One group of LCA students felt that guidance at junior cycle stage was not a necessity (Rosendale). This view was echoed by LCE students in Laurel Park who did not receive advice until in their (compulsory) Transition Year:

> You'd go silly if you started thinking about it [career choice] in third year. It's enough to try and cope with it in sixth year never mind third year. (LCE students, Laurel Park).

In sum, the case-study schools differed in terms of their approach to providing guidance at junior cycle level. In general, students were dissatisfied with the advice and guidance they had received on subject choice because they felt they knew too little about the subjects to make considered choices and did not know what subjects were required to access certain third-level courses.

5.4 PROVISION AT SENIOR CYCLE

The case-study schools varied in whether guidance provision consisted of regular classes for (groups of) sixth years, occasional classes or an appointment-based system. In just over half (eight) of the case-study schools, Leaving Certificate students had a regular class, usually once weekly, with the Guidance Counsellor. In these schools, regular classes were usually supplemented by individual appointments with the Guidance Counsellor. However, the schools varied in whether students could make appointments "on demand" or whether appointments were on a one-off basis to discuss CAO applications or aptitude test results. One school had occasional classes supplemented by an appointment system whereby students were allocated one appointment but could make further appointments themselves. In four of the case-study schools, the nature of guidance provision depended on the Leaving Certificate programme taken by students. In two schools, LCA students had regular guidance classes with an appointment-based system for LCE students. In two other schools, LCA and LCVP students had a weekly class supplemented by individual appointments while LCE students had only occasional classes and individual appointments. Two of the case-study schools had an appointment-based system with compulsory appointments for students in one of the schools.

Students were asked about the kinds of issues which were covered in their guidance classes or during their appointments with the Guidance Counsellor. The dominant focus of classes/meetings was on providing information and guidance on (applying for) third-level courses; students in almost all (14) of the schools mentioned that their class/meeting covered CAO applications, two-thirds of the schools organised visits to colleges during open days while three-fifths of schools had talks from college representatives. In contrast, PLC and FÁS courses were mentioned in only a small number of schools. Careers were mentioned separately from course applications in six of the case-study schools with visits from employers organised in five of these schools. Students in two schools also mentioned specific preparation for interviews. Where schools provided more than one Leaving Certificate programme, provision for LCA students was seen as focusing more on careers rather than post-school courses. In three-fifths of the schools, students reported that aptitude tests were used to give them guidance on the appropriate course and career choices. In one school, students had done a structured guidance project in fifth year. Other issues covered include the use of computer packages on careers or the internet (seven schools[9]) and study skills programmes (three schools).

In four of the case-study schools, students reported that the content of provision was flexible with the Guidance Counsellor being open to the students' suggesting topics to be covered in class:

---

[9] However, it should be noted that many students mentioned limited access to computers during school hours with many using their own computers at home to research their course and career choices.

Interviewer: Did you get the opportunity to suggest what you cover [in class]?

Yeah, if you ask a question about something he [Guidance Counsellor] would go over that with the whole class.

Yeah, if there was something specific you wanted you would go yourself to him. (LCE students, Laurel Park).

She [Guidance Counsellor] asks us all if there is anything we want.

She wouldn't just start, a lot of us let her know which way we are heading. So she wouldn't do something we are not interested in doing, she only focuses on the stuff we want to do. (LCA students, Maplewood).

Students differed in their levels of satisfaction with guidance provision with groups of students divided between those who were broadly satisfied with guidance (with some provisos) and those who were generally dissatisfied. In Laurel Park, students were broadly satisfied with the guidance they had received; attending careers exhibitions and having speakers come in to the school were seen as particularly helpful:

Yeah, I was lost apart from the careers exhibition.

Yeah, it was great.

And you don't have to pay any money for the information.

You might want to do something and then you find out what it is and you change your mind like.

It narrows down the options.

You can talk to the speakers about the colleges. They give you an idea about what's in the college. (LCE students, Laurel Park).

These positive perceptions were also related to the Guidance Counsellor being seen as approachable:

If you want advice the Guidance Counsellor is always there like, you can have a word with her, she always has time for you. (LCA students, Laurel Park).

In the remainder of the "satisfied" group of students, their satisfaction was qualified by their dissatisfaction with some aspects of guidance provision. First, while broadly satisfied, some students would have liked more time devoted to guidance. Second, some students would have preferred to be given guidance at an earlier stage. In Rosendale, for example, the appointment-based system was seen as very helpful in terms of completing CAO applications and students were happy with the choices they had made:

> Interviewer: So when you were making choices regarding the CAO, did you get much help?
>
> Yeah, we got a lot of help. She [Guidance Counsellor] went through every inch of it, really helpful.
>
> Interviewer: So you had a few sessions?
>
> Yeah.
>
> Yeah.
>
> She would give you as much time as she could provide, as you want. (LCE/LCVP students, Rosendale).

However, students would have liked more help and guidance at the fifth year stage. Similarly in Seaview, students were broadly satisfied with senior cycle provision (mainly because the Guidance Counsellor was seen as approachable) but would have liked to receive advice and information at an earlier stage:

> She [Guidance Counsellor] was always there if you needed to call to her, if you couldn't understand something, even on the corridor you could ask her straight away like and she'd have no problem.
>
> It should be maybe earlier in the year that it's sorted out so when it comes to filling out forms, you're going to be more sure of what order your subjects are going in and how to go about just simple stuff like all the formalities of getting your CAO form in. (LCE students, Seaview).

Third, a segment of students reported that they were satisfied with the advice they were given on courses and careers but dissatisfied with guidance on subject (and programme) choice within the school system. LCA students in Maplewood, for example, were positive about the Guidance Counsellor and the career advice they had received; however, they felt that they had not been fully informed about the LCA programme before-hand and some of the students would have liked more information on post-LCA course options. In Ashfield Park, students were broadly satis-fied with the advice on post-school options; however, they were dissatis-fied with advice on subjects and levels and some mentioned inadequate information about application deadlines. Similarly, students in Cherry-field View saw the Guidance Counsellor as approachable but were dis-satisfied with the lack of advice on subject choice.

In the second group of schools, students were broadly dissatisfied with guidance provision in their school. Firstly, some students were dis-satisfied with the amount of time spent on guidance and the difficulty in securing individual appointments with the Guidance Counsellor:

> Like I had one idea in my head all the time but I wasn't sure, I wanted to see what else was there like, not just the one thing. But it was hard like to get talking to the Guidance Counsellor one-to-one. It's hard because she has other classes. You can only meet with her once a week and then it's only for about twenty minutes, if you are lucky. (LCE students, Beechwood Square).

In Beechwood Square and Whitefield, a number of students had gone to private Guidance Counsellors outside school because of their dissatisfac-tion with provision in the school. Secondly, a number of students were dissatisfied with the advice they had received on subject choice, mainly because they had not chosen the subjects they needed for the third-level courses they would like to do (see above). Thirdly, a number of students were dissatisfied with the information they had received on available courses and careers and felt that guidance was overly focused on CAO applications. In Maplewood, for example, provision was seen as inade-quate by LCE students with too much focus on sixth year and little pro-vision at an earlier stage. Students in this school were dissatisfied with the amount of information they received on subject choice and course options, especially non-CAO options:

> I think . . . it's preferred that you do a course on the CAO. They want everyone to go to CAO courses. PLC is like last resort. A lot of people are quite happy with PLC, or even FÁS courses, we are not told about them at all. I don't think FÁS courses are hardly mentioned. Like you could do a FÁS course but then they go straight back to CAO.

> Especially for people who wouldn't be that interested in college. They are not told about those things. (LCE students, Maplewood).

In Beechwood Square, for instance, the focus of provision was seen as being on the mechanics of the CAO application process rather than on providing broader assistance with career choices:

> The CAO like, some of us did get advice on what we wanted to do but it was more on the actual filling out of the form, like, we weren't told what courses we wanted for whatever we wanted to do. So there was so much more to do like, to research.

> You don't have the time to do that yourself. (LCE students, Beechwood Square).

Many students, particularly those who wanted a non-mainstream course or career, felt they were not given enough information on the available courses and careers:

> It's [provision] very broad, you can't focus on any one thing. You have to decide yourself what course you want to do. The teacher just goes over, here is the CAO, you fill it up or pick your course, they don't go through it with you – here is the best course for you.

> Yeah, it's just general advice about the courses.

> Like we would have heard about two or three careers after we filled out the CAO form which we didn't know about when we were filling it out, that was stupid, we should have known about them before. (LCVP students, Whitefield).

College open days, for example, were only seen as being of help if students were already clear about what they wanted to do:

> We went to the Higher Options which I thought was really good but it wasn't good if you didn't know what you wanted to do. If you did-

n't know where you wanted to go it wasn't useful at all. (LCE students, Beechwood Square).

Some criticism also centred on the personality of the Guidance Counsellor. In Willow Grove, students felt they were not given as much advice as in other schools and the Guidance Counsellor was not seen as very approachable:

> She would never say you can go and talk to her. (LCVP students, Willow Grove).

Similarly, in Seaview and Chestnut Drive, the Guidance Counsellor was criticised for being overly-directive and focusing on a narrow range of career/course options:

> It would be better if we had a teacher that's going to help you find out what you want to do rather than tells you what you should do. (LCA students, Seaview).

> He doesn't give much information, you need more information, what you want to do, if I want to go into the army, just fill out a form, nothing else like.

> He never gave me any brochures on the home economics, I had to send away for them and my home economics teacher got them for me. (LCE students, Seaview).

In some of the schools, student satisfaction with guidance provision was related to the type of Leaving Certificate programme they were taking. In Laurel Park and Maplewood, LCA students felt that they were better prepared for life after school than LCE students:

> For them [LCE students] it's all just books, it's more like we get to practice interviews, we do computers.

> It's all for you on a personal level, it's not get out the books all the time. We can have an easier time.

> They [LCE students] will just have knowledge, information they will never need.

> Interviewer: Would you have better preparation?

> Yeah, we had to do interviews for our projects so we are more pre-
> pared for interviews outside for jobs. We will be more confident.
> (LCA students, Laurel Park).

> Like my friends that are doing the normal Leaving they don't have
> nearly as much, nearly as much like work with the careers. They
> have like one or two meetings in the year.

> Interviewer: Do you think you are going to be better prepared than
> the other Leaving Cert students?

> Yeah, definitely.

> Yeah, we have done work experience like, they have part-time jobs
> but we have our part-time jobs and we have our work experience.
> (LCA students, Maplewood).

This view was also reported by students in Greenwood; however, these
students also felt that LCE students had been given more advice (in
terms of course choice and visiting speakers) than the LCA group.

In contrast, in Lawton Way LCE students were broadly satisfied with
the Guidance Counsellor and happy with the choices they had made
while LCA students were dissatisfied in relation to information on post-
LCA options and careers; they felt they should have been given more
guidance on obtaining employment:

> I think they should have like plans for when people are leaving, what
> they should do or give them more advice.

> Yeah, they should set people up, you know at the end of sixth year,
> set you up with a job so when you go out you get a job.

> Interviewer: So you think they should have given you more informa-
> tion?

> They should really because some people don't know what they're
> doing like, we're finished now in a few weeks, no one knows what
> they're doing really. (LCA students, Lawton Way).

Somewhat surprisingly, satisfaction levels among students did not appear
to be related to whether the school had low, medium or high levels of
guidance provision. However, where students expressed a preference

relating to the nature of provision, they tended to prefer one-to-one rather than class-based sessions:

> You definitely do learn more one-to-one.

> When you are in a class you are all there in a class and you just don't get anything from it. Then if they concentrate on one [topic] you don't get any time.

> If they gave us more individual attention they would be able to give better direction but because there are so many of us she doesn't know us personally. Not like the way your English or your Maths teacher knows you and your strengths, she wouldn't like have an idea. (LCE students, Maplewood).

> You can speak up when you're on your own rather than in a class.

> Because it was one on one you were going over stuff that only you were interested in so everything to do with you, you got all stuff from different colleges and went through all the CAO forms and whatever, the Guidance Counsellor here had little tests to do for you to see if you were really suited to what you were looking into. (LCE students, Seaview).

When asked for suggestions on improving guidance provision, students mainly mentioned more time allocated to guidance:

> I would have liked more [guidance] this year. If anyone wanted to talk to him [Guidance Counsellor] he doesn't have a lot of time, he tries to see everyone.

> Sometimes you would be waiting a week for important stuff. He just can't do it. (LCE students, Hills Road).

More information on different courses and career options was also mentioned:

> For careers, they really need courses, I am not saying she is a terrible guidance teacher because she is not but there is a lot more she should know. (LCE students, Maplewood).

The need for guidance at an earlier stage (both junior cycle and fifth year) was also mentioned, in keeping with remarks made above about subject and career choices:

> In second year they should start explaining [to] students how it works. People should know how the points system works. And what the CAO form is.
>
> And you can think about what you want to do.
>
> Yeah, exactly, it's too late in fifth year or sixth year. (LCE students, Maplewood).

In sum, the focus of guidance provision varied somewhat from school to school but was mainly directed at third-level course choices and application procedures. Students were fairly evenly divided between those who expressed qualified satisfaction with existing provision and those who were generally dissatisfied. Concerns centred on the absence of advice on subject choice, the lack of guidance before the sixth year stage, the lack of time devoted to guidance, a focus on a relatively narrow range of course and career options, and the approachability of the Guidance Counsellor.

5.5 WORK EXPERIENCE

Because of their participation on programmes such as Transition Year and Leaving Certificate Applied, many of the students interviewed (students from twelve groups in all) had taken part in work experience placements during their time at school. These placements can, in theory, be used to help students decide on their longer-term career plans. In practice, students were generally positive about their work experience placements. It was seen as a chance to experience what certain jobs were actually like, even if this meant that students changed their mind about certain careers as a result:

> I really wanted to do childcare and I did it twice for work experience and god I love kids but it's not for me. I didn't like it.
>
> It does help you decide what you want to do.

The work experience was good. It was good to show you that you are actually able to do the job. If we had done the normal Leaving Cert we probably would have gone to college not knowing like we know now. (LCA students, Maplewood).

That was the best part of LCA, the work experience, I always wanted to be a chef like and I done that last year and I found out I didn't like it and if I didn't do the work experience I wouldn't have known so that's the good part of it. (LCA students, Greenwood).

However, some students had more equivocal views about the value of work experience in helping shape their career plans. In Laurel Park, for example, students were positive about their Transition Year work experience but felt they would have preferred to do a placement in an area they were interested in pursing as a career:

When you are fourteen, you don't really know what you want to do so you are just going to ask for any kind of a job.

When you think back you think I only wish that what I want to do today I had've got work experiences. Like I did hairdressing for week and I wished that I had've done something in a travel agency or tourism.

You change your mind so much like.

Yeah, you think it's what you want. (LCE students, Laurel Park).

This view was echoed by those in Oakhill Way who felt that work experience was least useful for students who had no clear idea about what they wanted to do in the longer term.

LCA students in Laurel Park had mixed views about their work experience depending on the nature of the placement itself:

Interviewer: In terms of your work experience, do you think you learned much from it?

I did mine in bar work and then I did bar management after school so it gave me an idea of what it's like. And how hard and busy it is.

I didn't to be honest, I didn't get to learn what I wanted, I was supposed to be doing leisure and recreation, to have my own place, but they had me doing something totally different so I didn't get what I wanted out of it.

I went to a local school, I watched the baby class so it was very good, I got to sit down with different children and teach them stuff, and learn what level they are at and how to question using rhymes and that, it's very interesting. So then the teacher is only out of college two years and she was telling me what she did and how she got to where she is. (LCA students, Laurel Park).

While work experience was broadly positive in its perceived influence on career choices, it should be noted that access to placements depended on the senior cycle programme taken by students with no work experience for Leaving Certificate Established students who had not taken Transition Year. Students in two of the schools suggested that work experience would also be useful for students who had not taken part in any specific programme.

5.6 SUPPORT STRUCTURES FOR STUDENTS

Students were also asked about the extent to which they saw their school as a supportive environment and if they would approach anyone in the school for help with a personal problem.

In most cases, students reported that they would be much more likely to go to family and friends with a problem and would be reluctant to talk to anyone in the school, including the Guidance Counsellor. Where school personnel were mentioned as a potential source of help, these included the Chaplain, Year Head, Class Tutor or individual subject teachers, depending on the school. In only three cases did students feel they could go to the Guidance Counsellor with a personal problem. In two schools (Laurel Park and Lawton Way, both disadvantaged schools), there appeared to be a "whole school" approach to providing support with students reporting that teachers were proactive in helping students with difficulties:

Sure if there was something wrong, the teachers would notice it.

If someone died in your family, one of the teachers would come up and they'd say are you alright?

> They'd notice, they'd know what's going on. (LCE students, Lawton Way).

In two of the schools, students mentioned that there was a specific person, a counsellor, who dealt with personal problems. However, students in Laurel Park seemed reluctant to go to the counsellor, although they did seem to prefer the fact that the guidance and counselling roles were separate:

> You have a choice really, one teacher for your school problems and you don't want them to get mixed up. (LCE students, Laurel Park).

Similarly, in Maplewood, there was a specific counsellor but students felt there were difficulties with accessing counselling and many students had not been aware of the counsellor's existence:

> Sometimes she is not there like. You can't turn round and say well I think I might have a problem in two weeks' time. There might be something in two weeks I better make an appointment. If something happens you need to go to them straight away. But it's not possible.

> I didn't know we had a counsellor.

> I was going to go and it was like yeah, you can see her in two weeks.

> You can't put off the breakdown for two weeks. (LCE students, Maplewood).

Even where no specific provision had been made for a designated counsellor within the school, many students expressed a preference for a separation between the roles of counsellor and teacher, considering it easier to talk to someone who was not a teacher and being concerned about confidentiality issues with teachers:

> Interviewer: Would you be more likely to go to someone who isn't a teacher?

> Yeah.

> I think they [the teachers] would tell each other.

> And you don't have to face them [designated counsellors] every day.

They [teachers] would think we are different. Or some of them might. (Junior Cert students, Maplewood).

You wouldn't tell a personal problem to the Tutor because in class then if you tell them something in class then you would be thinking what they are thinking of it, I think it'd affect the teacher/student relationship sort of. (Junior Cert students, Cherryfield View).

Here you are afraid that if you do tell her something confidential she will tell the rest of the teachers.

Yeah, you wouldn't trust her.

I wouldn't trust anyone in the school.

I used to have a Guidance Counsellor and she was very good, you could actually talk to her. She mightn't have been the best for careers but you could talk to her. But now the Guidance Counsellor I wouldn't go near because I know anything I say to her would be said back to the other teachers. (LCE students, Beechwood Square).

I wouldn't go to anybody here . . . I would be afraid they would discuss it with someone else, they probably wouldn't but I would prefer if someone came in once or twice a week if you want to see them. (Fifth years/ LCE students, Chestnut Drive).

In terms of suggestions for improving support structures in the school, many students mentioned they would like to see a designated counsellor or someone specific to deal with personal problems in their school. Students in Greenwood also mentioned they would have liked more support on coming into first year:

Interviewer: Would you like there to be more support for students?

At the start, yeah, when you're starting off in secondary school for students.

Interviewer: You think there needs to be more there?

Yeah, because it's a bit scary, when you come in, your first day in the place, 600 students walking around.

Interviewer: And you don't get much?

No, you're into it straight away. (Junior Cert students, Greenwood).

Students in Lawton Way expressed the need for help in coping with day-to-day life, for example, through drugs and alcohol awareness and sex education programmes; they also felt that depression was an issue for many students with the need for support for these students:

> A lot of people get depressed and they won't show it out but inside, you wouldn't know the way some students go on at home.
>
> Especially in fifth and sixth year.
>
> They keep saying after Leaving Cert and each teacher is saying that, it's putting more and more pressure.
>
> There's more pressure put on you.
>
> Some people can't handle pressure.
>
> Yeah that's what I'm saying some people can handle it, but some people go off the wall. (LCE students, Lawton Way).

In general, students felt they had little say in the running of the school, even where there was a student council in place:

> I know we can't run the school but we need to know a lot more about what's going on.
>
> We need to have our say as well. It's a dictatorship.
>
> It's one sided.
>
> You are not given a chance to say what you think and what you think they should change. You have to go of your own accord. (LCE students, Laurel Park).

In sum, students tended to be reluctant to approach anyone in the school for help with personal problems. However, many argued that schools should provide such support through a designated counsellor who was separate from the teaching staff.

5.7 SUMMARY AND DISCUSSION

An important aspect of the current study considers the views of students themselves both at the time of being in school and subsequent to leaving school. Findings from the national school leavers' survey data (and the case study data) indicate a strong reliance on external sources of advice among young people, particularly advice from parents, in making post-school educational and labour market decisions. A reliance on external sources of advice is particularly strong among early school leavers suggesting the need for greater guidance provision for pre-Leaving Certificate groups (in line with the findings of the previous chapter), particularly for those at risk of early leaving and the need to adequately inform parents of the options and choices open to students in school and the implications of these choices.

Findings from the case study analysis suggest some discrepancy between student's accounts of their guidance experiences and views expressed by key school personnel, although such discrepancies may relate to the timing of the national survey (completed several months prior to the case study analysis) and student perceptions or understanding of what counts as guidance. Overall, junior cycle students varied in their experiences of guidance, although many were critical of the information they received on the content of senior cycle subjects and the subject requirements of third level courses. At senior cycle level, while some were broadly satisfied with the guidance they had received (often where the Guidance Counsellor was seen as approachable), others were less satisfied: some were critical of the information they received on senior cycle subjects and programmes, while others would have liked more information and advice on post-school options, particularly options outside of the CAO system and non-mainstream courses and careers.

Chapter Six

TENSIONS FOR SCHOOLS IN GUIDANCE DELIVERY

6.1 INTRODUCTION

Analysis of the case study data revealed four areas which posed a certain tension and diversity across schools in the nature and effectiveness of the guidance and support services offered to their students. The first section of this chapter explores the extent to which there is a whole school approach to guidance and student support. The discussion then moves on to describe the nature of the school's role in providing personal/social support and counselling to students. The following section relates to the nature and adequacy of external support services and the fifth section relates to issues around the professional identity and training of Guidance Counsellors. Section Six provides a summary and discussion.

6.2 WHOLE SCHOOL APPROACH?

Various policy documents point to the need for a collaborative approach to guidance provision in second-level schools. Such an approach is evident, for example, in the 1992 Green Paper:

> While Guidance Counsellors have a central role to play in this (guidance) process, it is important that the provision of guidance should be seen as a school-wide responsibility, involving the collaboration of the school administration, the Guidance Counsellor and the other teachers. (p. 107).

The case-study schools varied in their approach to involving non-guidance teaching staff in guidance and pastoral issues. Three schools seemed to have more positive attitudes towards teacher involvement and a more pro-active approach to involving staff. The following quotes provide a good example of the way in which such greater integration can be achieved. Both quotes demonstrate high levels of interaction between key staff members.

> I couldn't sing the praises of the staff here [enough] . . . the Principal, very supportive and understanding. Then I meet very regularly with the learning support, the guidance teachers . . . And the counsellor we have is so helpful, as are the other staff and so willing to meet parents, etc. . . . and it's a wonderful support for me. (HSCL Officer, Ashfield Park).

> The Guidance Counsellor would integrate very much with the Year Heads and we also have a weekly, what we call learning support meeting where the Guidance Counsellor would attend . . . there would be integration there whereby they would meet with those people regularly so students at risk would be clearly identified and discussed. There would be a two-way flow. (Principal, Laurel Park).

These more "teacher-inclusive" schools (the two GEI schools and one other school) had initiated team-based programmes drawing on a range of teachers to address issues such as bullying and student self-esteem.

The remaining schools were less positive about the nature and extent of collaboration among staff regarding guidance and support. This seemed to result in a situation where members of staff were operating in isolation, which ultimately has implications for the adequacy of support available to students.

> Interviewer: To what extent would there be co-ordination between staff in the delivery of guidance and support?

> Deputy Principal: To be honest it wouldn't be great. That would be [the] different roles we all play. [Name of GC] would do one thing and I would do another, we don't cross over but we do have huge effort. Then you get some that just won't cooperate but you get that in every walk of life. (Chestnut Drive).

> Interviewer: In your view how adequate are the support structures for students in this school?

Guidance Counsellor: I would say they are fairly inadequate.

Interviewer: Why would you say that?

Guidance Counsellor: Because they are not coordinated, there is a lack of coordination. There is never a meeting of the support services. (Riverbank).

In some cases, members of staff appeared unsure of the role of the Guidance Counsellor and their status in the pastoral area and in the school generally. Such lack of clarity caused a certain level of tension between the staff and meant that guidance was not being delivered in a fashion that would maximise its effectiveness and utility to students.

. . . according to the guidelines from the Education Act . . . I was interpreting it that the Guidance Counsellor would co-ordinate the pastoral care in the school. There is a tension there and it hasn't been resolved. . . . Certainly according to the documentation I am getting from the NCGE and based on the Education Act the guidance area has an overall responsibility to the pastoral care, the coordination of pastoral care in the school. (Guidance Counsellor, Riverbank).

Interviewer: To what extent would you get an opportunity to share your guidance experiences with other staff members?

Guidance Counsellor: None. Only in conversation or in passing, it would be nothing formal . . . I think that it should be more of a whole school effort plan. Rather than almost an ad-hoc basis. There is no big policy surrounding the guidance area in school, I feel maybe it could be an area for growth in our school. (Beechwood Square).

Many schools saw the lack of co-ordination regarding guidance and the lack of awareness of the role of the Guidance Counsellor as an area needing attention.

. . . [the] staff needs to be more aware of the role of the Guidance Counsellor. And maybe I think work as part of a team, they [the Guidance Counsellor] can be very isolated as it is now. There is a perception there that it's all about CAO. To broaden the awareness, make staff more aware of what the role is. That needs to be done. (Principal, Beechwood Square).

It is evident from these schools that a clear and visible plan should be in place specifying each individual's role and the responsibilities of all staff members within the guidance and pastoral care domains. In addition to the lack of clarity about the role of staff in guidance and pastoral areas and the absence of a school/guidance plan, many school personnel identified time to meet as a factor hindering greater staff co-operation and co-ordination. Furthermore, as seen from the quote below, there is a perceived lack of time allocated to the pastoral care team, with the result that some students are not getting the support they need.

> I think time should be given to that pastoral care team working and examining the difficulties that are out there for kids. . . . I think some of the kids do suffer in silence because we're not, maybe a lack of communication, being passed, that's why I feel if the time was there for Tutors and myself and Year Heads to meet for half an hour and to say so and so is having difficulty, so and so's granny has died . . . (Chaplain, Greenwood).

Even one of the GEI schools, which had quite positive views of their guidance service, saw a need for greater collaboration between the Guidance Counsellors and wider staff, allowing a two-way flow of information.

> [there is a need] . . . for greater interaction between our Guidance Counsellors and staff on a more regular basis to feed back more often on students' needs or just to bring about an increased awareness of that. (Principal, Laurel Park).

Such awareness of guidance and a wider staff understanding of the area were seen as particularly important in the context of potentially sensitive issues emerging and possible implications for disclosure. One school, for example, noted that a staff member had given incorrect advice to a student regarding the confidentiality of information she had revealed. However, opinions were somewhat divided in terms of the extent to which all staff should have training in issues to do with the personal and social well-being of students. Staff training in general social/personal issues was seen as valuable and important in some schools.

. . . we need training in that whole area. I know there are courses that they have gone on this year and some of them have been fantastic. Especially the SPHE that was done in the last three years. It has been invaluable. I think you know teachers even if they are not teaching SPHE they can benefit from that. (Deputy Principal, Hills Road).

Interviewer: Are there any other services you would like to see?

Guidance Counsellor: Another service would be to train teachers, a lot of teachers have all these skills to help kids but they don't realise it. [It would be important] to train teachers.

Interviewer: To help students?

Guidance Counsellor: Yes, even to do the basics of counselling students. (Rosendale).

However, others were wary of the extent to which short-term training could equip teachers to deal with serious issues.

I don't know what you can give general teachers that would enable them to be confident in dealing with counselling issues, I don't know if a day or two training is sufficient, you are so fearful now of doing anything . . . we are called upon to be lots of different things without any protection against any allegation that might be made . . . not two or three days training. That isn't sufficient. That doesn't qualify you for anything. (Principal, Whitefield).

Overall, however, as noted earlier, there was recognition of the need for a whole school approach and response to serious issues that arise, at least from the point of view of raising awareness of the issues and identifying a unified staff response when problems emerge.

Well certainly in the whole area of suicide and issues related around that . . . that they have training or whatever it might be to take on that issue, so that we know what to do and how to respond when that happens. . . . I just feel that it's not seen maybe as urgent as I think it should be because we've had situations where there's been big trage-dies and we've really gone on instinct and I think in some cases peo-ple didn't know how to respond . . . we need a whole staff response. (Chaplain, Greenwood).

6.2.1 Perceptions of guidance

As was evident from the previous section, within the case study schools Guidance Counsellors, as well as school management, often observed difficulties in terms of wider staff understanding and perceptions of the role of the Guidance Counsellor. While some of this related to a lack of awareness of the actual role of the Guidance Counsellor, in other cases this reflected perceived negative staff opinion relating to the non-teaching status of some Guidance Counsellors, the freedom to determine their own time schedules and their allocation of office facilities.

> . . . two of the biggest problems that come up all the time in schools are Guidance Counsellors and Chaplains, why because neither of them are timetabled, now that's a mind set, but that mind set has to be dealt with because among the teaching staff in schools Guidance Counsellors are generally very resented. (Principal, Seaview).

> . . . teachers tend to look on the Guidance Counsellor as someone a bit different, not one of the lads . . . whether that is a weakness or not I don't know, I know it happens in other schools. (Guidance Counsellor, Lawton Way).

Conversely, in a number of schools guidance had a more positive profile in the school, which seemed to create a more positive working environment for the Guidance Counsellor. In particular, where guidance is seen as valued and facilitated, particularly by school management, this was seen to greatly boost the work of the Guidance Counsellor.

> . . . [something that] management would strongly support is the importance of guidance. . . . I think that has been the greatest facility for me and my work. I have been given this room, it's a brand new office . . . you name it they have facilitated because they see the importance of the subject. And they have allowed the flexibility . . . with meetings, one-to-one meetings with students, and I think that is really helping. (Guidance Counsellor, Cherryfield View).

6.3 ROLE OF SCHOOLS IN PERSONAL/SOCIAL SUPPORT

6.3.1 Introduction

The Department of Education and Science (2005) set out a broad framework for the role of schools in "counselling". They maintain that "counselling should be available on an individual basis to assist students in their personal and social, educational and career development":

> In cases where students require personal counselling over a protracted period of time or counselling of a therapeutic nature, Guidance Counsellors, given their other time commitments and unless they have appropriate qualifications for working with such students, should refer such cases to outside agencies.

The issue of the role schools play and should play in the area of personal support and counselling for students arose in all of the case study schools. The issue was seen as particularly pertinent in the context of wider societal changes, changing family structures and the implications for students' social and emotional wellbeing. As one Deputy Principal commented:

> The need [for personal support/counselling] seems to grow exponentially from year to year. I think that is true of society, not just us. (Deputy Principal, Whitefield).

Among the issues of concern to school personnel were the expertise of staff and Guidance Counsellors to deal with the social/psychological concerns of students, the extent to which students would be comfortable to approach school personnel with personal issues, the extent to which schools should have a moral obligation to address the social and emotional concerns of students and the actual role schools are best placed to play – prevention, identification and referral and/or therapeutic.

As discussed in Chapter Four, Guidance Counsellors vary widely in the extent to which they adopt a holistic or dual role encompassing career/educational guidance and personal counselling or a role more narrowly focused on career preparation. For some, a greater focus on career guidance was seen to reflect prioritisation in a context of very limited resources. Others did not see their qualifications or expertise as allowing them to offer a "counselling" service to their students. For a number of Guidance Counsellors, their role had been defined, either by themselves, predecessors or school management, as one serving the career guidance needs of students.

> . . . in my two years I have only seen one person for personal coun-
> selling and that was by accident, it came out in a [career] guidance
> session. . . . I don't think it's seen as my area. I'm the careers teacher
> I think rather than Guidance Counsellor. (Guidance Counsellor,
> Beechwood Square).

Schools also varied in their role and emphasis on personal/social support and counselling for their students. Some saw counselling as central to the needs of their students and fulfilled this role either through the activities of the Guidance Counsellor, through the employment of specialist coun-sellors/psychotherapists or through the use of third level counselling stu-dents seeking work placements. Seaview availed of students from Trinity College, who came to the school two days per week, seeing 15-16 stu-dents per week. Such counselling was seen to play an important role:

> it would be a lot of prevention [work that] would take place . . . they
> see us [school staff] as authority figures telling them what to do all
> the time . . . [whereas] they are free to discuss their problems in a
> non judgmental way [with these counselling students]. (Principal,
> Seaview).

6.3.2 Personal and social issues emerging

Schools reported a wide range of problems experienced by students. Among the more frequently mentioned were issues around family break-down and family structure, substance abuse, mental health (depression, eating disorders and suicide), bullying, pregnancy and peer relationships.

> Interviewer: What would be the main kinds of issues that come up?

> Guidance Counsellor: Mostly family. Break-ups, separation. Suicide
> is a huge one in this area. We have had about 13 cases where parents
> committed suicide. So that would be a big issue. [There are always
> the] usual grief issues. Somebody's behaviour issues, they would be
> having a hard time at home and then just within here just trying to

> maintain some kind of relationship and be as positive with them.
> (Whitefield).

Boys were often seen to present with different issues to girls or at least their problems manifested in different ways. Boys experiencing difficulties were often found to display outwardly negative behaviour while girls would be more likely to display more subtle withdrawal, although they were more likely to speak to a friend.

> Boys they tended to show negative behaviour . . . non-compliance, lack of authority, discipline, lack of respect for structured authority. And could give loads of cues. . . . [What about girls?] It would be obvious but not in the same way, girls would get upset. Girls would talk to a friend and a friend would come and say Miss I think someone needs to talk to you . . . there would be signs of anger but not in the very obvious way [like boys]. (Guidance Counsellor, Ashfield Park).

In many cases, students themselves approach the Guidance Counsellor for an appointment. In other cases, students are referred through their Tutor, Year Head or school management.

> The students approach me to make an appointment, I would say in 90 per cent of the cases they would just knock on the door and I wouldn't actually know some of the times why they're coming so they would just turn up and ask for an appointment. Sometimes I get a note under my door as well. (Guidance Counsellor, Laurel Park).

In some cases, problems being experienced by students manifest in disciplinary issues. A number of schools offer personal support to students on suspension with a view to addressing any underlying personal concerns.

> I get a lot of referrals from Class Tutors and Year Heads. Principal, Deputy Principal also refers any student back from suspension or red report, which is the highest disciplinary system. So they feel its not just a disciplinary measure, its support as well. So they are referred to me and, if possible, I would see them on a weekly basis until they feel they can go back into the class. (Guidance Counsellor, Ashfield Park).

Schools with a more whole-school approach to pastoral care (see section 6.2) were more likely to identify a range of school personnel students could approach with problems, which in many cases would then be referred to the Guidance Counsellor or Chaplain. This approach was often considered to be more effective, particularly where students were perceived as reluctant to approach a designated staff member (typically the Guidance Counsellor).

> They are reluctant to go to the Counsellor. Even if you meet the girls here and ask them would you go and talk to your form teacher about something, no, no, they won't. (Principal, Beechwood Square).

While some students were seen as willing to approach the Guidance Counsellor or other staff members with personal concerns, key personnel in a number of schools felt that their students were reluctant to do so. Indeed students themselves expressed such reluctance, as discussed in Chapter Five. There was some recognition of the potential benefits of a non-staff member fulfilling such a role, allowing students to talk in confidence about concerns, without fear of other teachers learning of their concerns. Furthermore, students were seen to find it difficult to talk to teachers about such personal issues when these teachers are acting in a disciplinary capacity within the classroom:

> I think it's a good idea that an outsider comes in because she has a low profile in the school. Students . . . are slow to come to a teacher because if something is very painful or confidential they are worried they might be too exposed if they tell a teacher. . . . If you have a counsellor whose role is purely counselling and if they don't have the discipline role they are more forthcoming. (Guidance Counsellor, Rosendale)

More generally, the issue of conflict between disciplinary and more supportive roles emerged. While on the one hand the majority of Guidance Counsellors have a teaching role and as such must act in a disciplinary capacity where necessary and ensure an orderly classroom environment, on the other hand, in their position as Guidance Counsellor, they are most effective if seen as supportive, non-critical and generally outside of the disciplinary process.

> One thing that is vitally important for Guidance Counsellors is that they are not seen as disciplinarians and that is one of the dilemmas for a career guidance teacher. If you want to be seen as a disciplinarian in one class . . . how are they going to come to you if they have a problem. (Guidance Counsellor, Willow Grove).

The issue of student willingness to approach (designated) staff members with issues of personal concern is discussed further in Chapter Five where focus groups with students in the case study schools explore students' own experiences of, and views on, the matter.

6.3.3 Need for more personal/social support

Most of the case study schools expressed the need for additional personal/social support for students and identified the lack of such provision as a serious gap in the support of students with particular social/psychological concerns.

> . . . if we had any hope of getting a second career Guidance Counsellor, with a strong emphasis on counselling. . . . in any school I feel now there should be some allowance for a counsellor. It's a rural area but unfortunately in the latter years these problems are creeping in. (Deputy Principal, Chestnut Drive).

> The counsellor side of career guidance it doesn't really get touched unless the kids themselves go to the career guidance teacher. Because I don't think the time is there for that. . . . And the system doesn't allow that. (Deputy Principal, Beechwood Square).

While the call for greater personal/social support for students was widespread, there was some recognition that needs were likely to vary across schools, depending on the prevalence of social and economic problems in the catchment area.

> . . . I think it really depends on the school and the needs of the student's area. There are some schools and there is absolutely no doubt [that there is little need], like here it could be combined with the role of careers teacher. . . . In my last employment I feel they should have been separated and [the school should] have three people on each one [careers and counselling]. (Guidance Counsellor, Cherryfield View).

This was also reported in an earlier study (Ryan, 1993) which found that the amount of time devoted to personal counselling varied in different parts of the country – counsellors working in urban schools reported that they spent significantly more time on personal counselling than their counterparts in schools located in small towns and rural areas (p. 11). This may relate to variations in the socio-economic composition of schools in urban and rural areas and the needs of students.

6.3.4 Role for school

While some schools did offer students counselling support, either from existing school personnel such as the Guidance Counsellor or through the employment of specialist counsellors, other schools saw their role as one of identification of problems and referral.

> Yes we had some private issues, but [name of Guidance Counsellor] would refer on. I might say to her, look, your counselling is counselling so far, we are not trained to go further than that. (Principal, Ashfield Park).

> I feel as a Guidance Counsellor I am not fully equipped to do that kind of work. I am not properly trained. The Department don't pay for supervision. And I just feel it wouldn't be professional for me to do therapeutic counselling. I would do first line counselling, maybe picking up problems, make referrals. If it's somebody who needs support or help with dealing with stress I can do that but there are deeper issues. I am not trained to deal with them and I am very conscious of that. (Guidance Counsellor, Maplewood).

Many Guidance Counsellors noted that they treaded a fine line between supporting students and actually counselling them on serious issues. They were wary of engaging in counselling per se within the school setting but they did see a role in referring them to specialist services and in monitoring and supporting them as they undertook more specialised counselling outside of school.

> . . . you have to kind of decide, one a referral, if it's not possible, you're not even competent to get into too much stuff and it's not even appropriate I think to be into very serious counselling on an long term basis with a kid in the school. . . . But you do have to bring them along to a point where you can monitor and support them, so to get that balance right. (Principal, Seaview).

> . . . we're very careful, I come from a background myself that the competency in counselling is a very serious matter and we're very

> conscious of the fact that we don't get caught with, get into areas
> where we're not qualified to deal with and that they must be referred.
> (Principal, Seaview).

Some also expressed concerns over public perceptions on the appropriateness of schools employing a Counsellor. The issue of what is the most
appropriate "site" for student counselling is an important one: while several of the schools held that such counselling can be undertaken on the
school grounds (with the employment of qualified counsellors in many
cases), others felt that such services should be offered outside of the
school setting.

> . . . while we have counsellors we haven't got people who are hugely
> qualified in counselling, but then again I don't know if any schools
> have. It's something that is a luxury, if someone happens to come
> your way, I don't think in a school of this size that they could put an
> ad in the paper looking for a trained counsellor. (Pastoral Care Co-
> ordinator, Beechwood Square).

> What are our parameters really, because if we are to do everything
> they say we should be doing are we a school at all? We have a lot of
> issues coming at us and they are complex . . . I still think we haven't
> got what maybe the real expert counsellors have. (Pastoral Care Co-
> ordinator, Beechwood Square).

Indeed a number of staff expressed concerns over the danger of "counselling" students without account being taken of the home context, suggesting that a more comprehensive family therapy/counselling set-up
would be more appropriate and beneficial.

> I suppose one of the problems I would have the thing with these kids
> is they are coming out of a family system and really if you are coun-
> selling someone separate from a system you need to be very careful
> how you manage it because that child has to go back into the system
> at home and while the child might be giving me a perception of a
> system the system might. . . . I wouldn't be aware of all the dynam-
> ics. (Guidance Counsellor, Chestnut Drive).

Overall, many interviews with key personnel drew attention to the dan-
gers of counselling students in a school setting. There were serious questions raised regarding the appropriateness of counselling students in a

school setting, removed from their family background. Such questions also concerned the issue of the role of a school and to what extent they have an obligation to address serious personal/social issues experienced by their students. In addition, many Guidance Counsellors questioned their ability, training and capacity to undertake a thorough counselling role. However, many identified the need to pick up problems at an early stage and consider schools to be in a unique position to play such a preventative role.

> Interviewer: What would you see as the main priorities for the future?

> . . . more time and as I said on an individual basis, to deal with people whose problems might not be seen as major but nevertheless needs counselling and advice. I think a lot of problems in schools, discipline problems stem from the fact that the relatively small problems don't get dealt with and then they become larger problems. (Principal, Oakhill Way).

> I think there is a very important role to be played, I think the department has to put money into educational psychology, this is a greater need and you get children in here at very early stages, their lives very messed up and they're just going into adolescence. (Principal, Seaview).

Indeed, a number of schools felt they were playing an effective preventative role in the early identification of problems and the availability of personal/social support to students.

> If the Guidance Counsellor can get in to prevent difficulties which someone can do if they have time to deal with first years in particular then you don't have the same problems, socially, education wise and personal problems later on. (Guidance Counsellor, Ashfield Park)

> In my first few years . . . I would have had a number of suicide attempts. [But now] at least there is somebody available to talk and that's known and it's out there, so lets hope it doesn't get as serious as it used to. (Guidance Counsellor, Laurel Park)

6.3.5 Separate counselling role?

Schools varied in their views on whether career guidance and counselling are best offered within the same role or separated into two distinct positions. Many school personnel felt the ideal situation would be the operation of separate career guidance and counselling roles:

> But I think actually guidance and counselling should be separate. Really the guidance is one kind of a job and counselling is totally different. It's a whole heap of work in the counselling. It's different today with kids. (Principal, Beechwood Square).

> Well I don't think you can do both. I don't think you can counsel and do career guidance. I think career guidance is a full time job. And that is for everybody in the school. As regards a counsellor it's a full time job. (Deputy Principal, Beechwood Square).

One school had separated the guidance into two distinct roles, guidance and counselling (Laurel Park). The availability of such a dedicated "counsellor" (with a qualification in psychotherapy) was seen to be very effective and of enormous benefit to students. The system also meant that one person was responsible for contact with external services and parents and allowed a more organised and structured response to needs as they arose, which had not been available previously.

> I suppose it's [the new counselling role has] been very effective, . . . any communication that arrives into the school to do with any of these services, or to do with students, I look after all of that so there's one person who knows what's going on . . . I suppose it just brings everything together really rather than very valuable bits of information being held by different people. (Guidance Counsellor, Laurel Park).

The benefits were also seen in the Guidance Counsellor not being placed in a discipline role and hence the danger of conflict between discipline and supportive roles (as noted earlier) did not emerge:

> . . . the dual role is a very difficult one to do. And as well as that this whole thing on discipline, discipline is still a difficult one, trying to negotiate that with students because really essentially my role here in

the school is not as a disciplinarian. (Guidance Counsellor, Laurel
Park).

6.3.6 Directions for the future

While schools and Guidance Counsellors largely determine the nature
and breadth of guidance counselling services offered to their students,
many argue that additional resources should be made available to Guidance Counsellors or other key school personnel who wish to pursue additional qualifications/training in specialist counselling/therapy areas. Al-
ternatively a number of schools contend that resources should be offered
to allow schools to employ the services of private specialist counsellors.
Ultimately school personnel and/or management may or may not consider the counselling of students to be within their remit or capacity and
individual schools and personnel must be given the option to make such
choices. In the event that they define their role as one of offering initial
counselling, or feel they have the skills and capacity to offer such counselling to students in immediate need of assistance, the resources should
be available. However, for the most part, the research suggests that
schools are best placed to identify students experiencing personal/social
difficulties and refer them on to specialist external services. However,
for such a referral role to be effective schools must have immediate and
effective external services available to call on when the need arises and
they must be aware of the nature of the support services available and the
key people to contact in the event of a need arising. The next section discusses schools' experiences with, and perceptions of, the external support services available.

6.4 WIDER SUPPORT: EXTERNAL SUPPORT SERVICES

If schools are to play an effective role in the identification of students
experiencing difficulties and referral of these students to specialised external support services, it would seem pertinent to consider the nature
and responsiveness/effectiveness of the external support services.

6.4.1 National Educational Psychological Service

Many of the external supports mentioned by Guidance Counsellors related to the services of the National Educational Psychological Service (NEPS), social services and health boards.

The majority of Guidance Counsellors emphasised difficulties in accessing NEPS services, including delays in NEPS responding and the long waiting times in actually getting access to the service.

> Well when you get them they are good. But they are difficult to get, they have their own resources problems. (Principal, Hills Road).

> . . . the big problem [with NEPS] I feel is the delay . . . it's very difficult to get back confirmation on what services you can get and get them in place. For the incoming students or whatever they can be slow. (Home School Community Liaison Officer, Ashfield Park).

In addition, some key personnel felt that the NEPS was too narrowly focused on educational needs, neglecting the psychological needs of students.

> . . . the difficulty there is that there is a difference between educational needs and psychological problems, you would have someone assessed on the basis of their educational deficiency and the psychological problems mightn't be dealt with. . . . The school psychologist has a particular brief – to assess educational needs. (Principal, Willow Grove).

When services were accessed, many felt the NEPS was offering an important service to schools and students. However, they did feel that the service was generally inflexible and did not always respond to genuine need.

> Interviewer: Would you think the support services are adequate?

> Guidance Counsellor: No, NEPS no way. Not at all. . . . one of the most frustrating things, the Department of Education won't accept data from the school, they need everything to be very precise, through assessment and we are waiting months for an assessor and the school is given a certain allocation and if something more urgent crops up one of the children already on the list has to be demoted to make way for that child. (Ashfield Park).

Others noted that where there was a need to draw on counselling services from the NEPS psychologist, such time was then taken from their allocation for testing-purposes.

> . . . we had two suicides last year . . . the local educational psychologist did come up and did do some counselling but . . . because she had been here for two days that time was then taken away from testing. . . . Because the fact those students needed counselling did not mean we didn't have students who needed to be assessed. (Deputy Principal, Whitefield).

The reliance on private provision was also apparent, both in the areas of private psychological assessment for learning difficulties and private counselling support for those experiencing personal/social difficulties. As noted earlier, a number of schools employed private counsellors/ psychologists, sometimes using resources from other school programmes, such as the School Completion Programme.

> Under our school completion . . . [we] bring in outside independent psychologists who we pay for various kids who were in dire straits and now that we have the money under the school completion we have set aside some money for that kind of intervention. (Principal, Seaview).

> . . . the reality is that some kids unless they can pay won't be able to get it [assessment]. And the vast majority of parents can't pay. . . . There's a lot of waiting lists. For them to go private it's quicker. (Principal, Rosendale).

Others obtained private (learning difficulty) assessments to secure exam exemptions.

> . . . there is an increasing reliance on private provision of counselling, etc. Especially with regards to where exemptions are sought in exams, it's now almost the norm to get a private psychologist report. (Principal, Oakhill Way).

6.4.2 Social services/health boards

As discussed above, a number of Guidance Counsellors presented their role as being one of referral to external support services, such as the social services and health boards. Some saw this "referral role" as expanding and occupying an increasingly important place in their work, while others saw it as something that they have become more aware of in recent times.

> . . . one of my most difficult days I think, about two weeks ago I had four cases I had to refer on to the health board in one day. So I think because my role has developed, what exists is coming more to the surface so maybe it's coming to my attention rather than getting more serious. (Guidance Counsellor, Laurel Park).

> . . . a lot of my work is actually now linked with child and adolescence psychiatry and also the GPs and the health board. So I've made a lot of links there so some students I might be working with, they also may be in other services. So there's a lot of, I suppose it's just developed, there's a lot of contact between the services. (Guidance Counsellor, Laurel Park).

Again Guidance Counsellors and other school personnel were critical of their experience with these services. In particular, difficulties surrounding access to the appropriate health board person and delays in response were widespread.

> I have been in touch with the health board quite a lot over the years for various students. And it's very, very, very time consuming. Very hard to get a social worker, it's very hard to get action. (Guidance Counsellor, Ashfield Park).

> . . . the waiting time is very long. If you go through public health or the Department of Education, you are waiting for so long. (Chaplain, Riverbank).

The response from the social services did however appear to vary according to the issue and the seriousness of the case.

A common issue in discussions of the social services was the difficulty in identifying and accessing the appropriate person. A number of Guidance Counsellors identified the need for an appropriate liaison person between schools and the social services/health boards.

> I think there is a gap . . . there is a huge gap in the area of a liaison person who understands our role as a school. Who understands we

are very limited and once someone has to be referred out I think
there should be a bridge, so we can understand each other's language. (Guidance Counsellor, Ashfield Park).

I came from the health board . . . so I would be familiar with the
health board structures and even I find it a labyrinth trying to track
down the appropriate person, that is very difficult. . . . Like if there is
a local social worker nobody ever knocks on our door and says we
are the person, we have to seek them out. . . . That takes a lot of time.
(Guidance Counsellor, Maplewood).

Those who appeared most satisfied with the support services had built up
an effective network of contacts in the relevant agencies.

I find them excellent now because I've built up a very good network
. . . I've one person in particular [social worker] who has been excellent, is constantly there available, has given me her mobile number
so I can contact her. I definitely find the service very, very good, I
must say. (Guidance Counsellor, Laurel Park).

Schools also drew on a wide range of other statutory and non-statutory
external services: GPs, Gardaí/Juvenile Liaison Officers, National Educational Welfare Board, voluntary groups (Barnardos, Rape Crisis Centre), religious-run services (Lucena Clinic), local youth service groups
and university staff/professional counsellors.

Guidance Counsellor: Here we have [county name] youth services
that we can refer students to. Now the problem there is waiting lists.

Interviewer: What sort of things would you refer for?

Guidance Counsellor: I would refer for behaviour, aggressive behaviour. Bereavement, kids who have lost somebody. Or even parental
break-up. (Rosendale).

I would have to say that the educational psychology Department in
[university name] have been very, very helpful. . . . To be fair to
them I can always pick up the phone and they will ring me back. If I
have a difficulty they will come out. (Guidance Counsellor, Willow
Grove).

6.4.3 Services required

Across nearly all interviews, staff emphasised the need for improved access to statutory services and reduced waiting periods.

> I think it would be great even if [name of Guidance Counsellor] and myself considered that a student needed counselling for example, that she could simply phone someone up and say this student needs more than I can give, then they [an outside professional] can see them after school. Obviously it's needed there and then not six months down the line. (Deputy Principal, Whitefield).

> We do have a lot of problems that aren't picked up on time. But you can't get someone when you need it, it has to be severe, you are like a fire brigade. (Deputy Principal, Rosendale).

Overall many argued for a more comprehensive and responsive support system for schools in dealing with students' social and emotional needs, particularly when addressing behavioural issues.

> I think greater provision [is needed], I mean a support system that would be there for us, we're dealing with students all the time and there's a limit to what you can do in a school situation with difficult students . . . it's nearly an ongoing support system that you would need for them . . . in school I feel we're not able to do it. (Guidance Counsellor, Greenwood).

More generally, key personnel suggested that schools and support services should place greater emphasis on student motivation and self-esteem and the reinforcement of positive behaviour.

> One type of service I would love to see would be groups who can come into the school and can do work with the classes. Or small groups, they will come into the school environment. . . . [Work] with the weaker kids, work on self-esteem, motivation, behaviour. (Guidance Counsellor, Rosendale).

Finally, the issue of the identification and awareness of supports available to schools arose frequently in the interviews. Many felt that services should be more easily identifiable – their role and the key contact people should all be clear to schools before an issue or problem arises.

. . . it needs to be clear-cut. There doesn't seem to be much link between the schools and social services like that, there is very little interaction until there is a problem. (Deputy Principal, Cherryfield
View).

I would like an improvement on the existing services and for them to
be more visible. I would like them to network with us, make contact
with us, let us know who they are, where they are, how we contact
them. And even to establish some kind of relationship with them.
(Guidance Counsellor, Maplewood).

6.4.4 Reliance on private services

As discussed earlier, across the board a large number of schools and students were substituting private for public services, particularly in the areas
of assessment and psychological and psychiatric support. One-third of the
case-study schools had, during the previous two years, employed the services of a private counsellor/clinical psychologist[10], the majority funded
through school resources (such as the school completion programme) or
from parents directly. This raises issues over equality of access and the
ability of some groups of parents to fund such private services.

A lot of students who would have needed it their families wouldn't
have been in a position whereas more financially capable parents
would have done it. (Guidance Counsellor, Ashfield Park).

Similar issues surround access to statutory psychological and psychiatric
services: lengthy waiting lists mean that in reality often it is only those
who can afford to pay who can access the necessary supports.

. . . we have two students now who, two sixth years actually who attend a psychiatrist, they had to be referred on but it costs parents an
awful lot of money, they can manage it for a while if need be but we
have had two sixth years actually who should be going to counselling and are not, parent is a single parent and can't manage it and if
you refer them to free counselling, teen counselling there's always a
waiting list. (Deputy Principal, Seaview).

---

[10] One school, participating in the GEI, indicated that they would like to employ the services of a private counsellor, but "are prohibited within the rules of the [GEI] scheme
from using our budget to hire in outside professional help".

> I would think we would try to get the state to do something but warn
> the parents it might take too long and then of course it does take too
> long. Then the ward would go to the parents and say really things are
> not good. It's important that they get this and you are going to have
> to pay. (Deputy Principal, Oakhill Way).

The reality was a strong reliance on private services, either employed
within the school or accessed outside of the school, usually through referral from the school.

6.5 PROFESSIONAL IDENTITY

A common issue in cross-national reviews of guidance services in
schools is the issue of the qualifications and training of Guidance Counsellors. On the one hand, training requirements vary given the varying
roles Guidance Counsellors play in different countries: in some Guidance Counsellors take a holistic role encompassing personal and social as
well as career guidance, in others their role is more narrowly focused on
career guidance. In many countries, however, Watts and Sultana (2003)
note that there is a need for stronger occupational structures in the career
guidance field, with current structures weak in comparison with those in
related professions. Often, they observe, qualifications from apparently
related fields – such as teaching and psychology – seem to be regarded
as proxies for guidance qualifications, without any verification of
whether they assure the requisite competencies or not.

There is also the issue of the diversity of people involved in the delivery of guidance and counselling support for students, particularly in a
more whole school approach as discussed earlier. The need to ensure
flexible delivery methods and broaden access to guidance needs to be
balanced with clarity over the role of guidance professionals within such
diversified delivery systems.

6.5.1 Professional status/qualifications

While the majority of the Guidance Counsellors in the case-study
schools had completed guidance counselling courses and were qualified
Guidance Counsellors (typically completing a graduate diploma in guidance and counselling, often on a two-year part-time basis), this was not

the case for all "Guidance Counsellors". In one school the Guidance Counsellor had initially come to the school as a resource teacher but was allocated to the guidance role upon arrival, although they had no formal qualifications in the guidance area. In fact, work by the NCGE (Audit in 1999-2000) found that 23 per cent of Guidance Counsellors working in second-level schools were listed as having qualifications other than Irish post-graduate qualifications in guidance counselling.

There was a certain amount of ambiguity among Guidance Counsellors as to the qualifications required to act as a Guidance Counsellor:

> . . . it's a grey area with the VEC as to whether they recognise me as qualified as a Guidance Counsellor. You don't necessarily have to have the qualification from what I discovered from my research, being onto the department, the Guidance Counsellors association and from what I can derive nobody could really give me a clear answer but it would appear on the VEC, when they look at your qualifications and they say you have done enough, you have enough experience in this area. (Guidance Counsellor, Cherryfield View).

Conversely, a number of Guidance Counsellors had completed additional more specialised training, mostly in the counselling area where they felt more specialised qualifications were essential for undertaking such work:

> I myself have gone on and done a higher diploma in psychotherapy two years ago and I'm doing my masters this year so I'll be a fully qualified psychotherapist as well. (Guidance Counsellor, Laurel Park).

However, as discussed later, some were critical of the financial assistance available from the Department of Education and Science to undertake such training.

6.5.2 In-service training

The vast majority of the Guidance Counsellors had attended in-service training, which in most cases was seen as valuable and useful. Guidance Counsellors felt they could benefit from one another's experiences and found this opportunity worthwhile.

> I find them [in-service courses] very valuable because you're hearing another slant on something, somebody else's experience, I think they're invaluable, I feel guilty about asking for time off but I think it's very important that we are aware and updated in those skills. (Guidance Counsellor, Greenwood).

In many cases, the value of in-service participation was seen in the opportunities it provided for networking and meeting up with other Guidance Counsellors, which was seen as particularly valuable in a context where most Guidance Counsellors are operating in isolation with the only contact with other Guidance Counsellors occurring outside of the school environment.

> They [the in-service courses] are good to keep one's spirit alive, to keep up the morale. In a school you are isolated, you are the only one that's doing it and you do need support from others from time to time. (Guidance Counsellor, Riverbank).

> Yes, I do [find in-service courses useful]. You are very much on your own in the school so even just to talk and have contact with other people doing the same thing makes a big difference. (Guidance Counsellor, Oakhill Way).

A number of interviewees suggested more concentrated blocks of training would be preferable and of greater benefit, particularly for Guidance Counsellors who had completed their initial training a considerable time ago.

> . . . it's 1980 when I did my course, I think there should be more in-service courses, not the token day here and there . . . I feel there should be comprehensive [training] rather than just a token thing. . . . every ten years certain groups should be given a week out of school to do this. . . . All of us who have training years ago need to be trained, upskilled (Guidance Counsellor, Willow Grove).

This could be seen to be particularly important in a context where only half of Guidance Counsellors working in schools have obtained their guidance qualifications since 1986 (NCGE Audit, 1999/2000).

Most schools appeared to facilitate such training participation – school management (Principals) recognised the value and importance of

in-service training for Guidance Counsellors and accepted the difficulties
and disruptions absences for training created.

> We would never stand in the way here of, despite the disruption it
> might cause, although sending a Guidance Counsellor off for a day
> doesn't cause a huge amount of dysfunction, it may have an impact
> on the amount of time they can spend with students but we have al-
> ways considered it's far more important to have teachers out there,
> in-touch and developing, you just put up with the inconvenience.
> (Principal, Laurel Park).

6.5.3 Further training

Guidance Counsellors were asked if they felt there were any areas where
they would like further training/skills. Two areas emerged as prominent
in their responses: counselling and psychology expertise/knowledge.
Some also mentioned the issue of professional support as a counsellor.

> I would probably like to have more formal qualifications in the area
> of counselling . . . I think that that is a potential weakness. (Guidance
> Counsellor, Cherryfield View).

> I think there is a lot more counselling issues coming up and I think
> Guidance Counsellors need personal support as in professional sup-
> port as a Guidance Counsellor for the issues that they have to deal
> with. That would be one thing that would be a must and I think it
> should be allocated and paid for by the department. (Guidance Coun-
> sellor, Ashfield Park).

A key concern expressed by Guidance Counsellors was the availability
of financial support to undertake additional and more specialised training. The need for financial support to undertake training was widely
mentioned.

> . . . the one thing that galls me is that when I genuinely do want to
> get the skills and pick up the skills but there's a financial block put in
> front of me and if I was trained I would have so much more to bring
> to the job. (Chaplain, Greenwood).

> I would love to do the masters but I think it's very unfair we have to
> pay for it ourselves, I really do. I would welcome more training. . . .
> If I was to do some specialised training in counselling, in an accred-

ited course, most of them are four to five thousand a year, I feel there
should be, if they want us to do that they should be paying for it.
(Guidance Counsellor, Maplewood).

While some had undertaken training at their own expense, others felt that
was not an option.

6.6 SUMMARY AND DISCUSSION

While an emphasis on a whole school approach to guidance and student
personal/social support is evident in policy documents, such an emphasis
was by no means a feature of all of the case study schools. There were
important issues over staff awareness of the role of the Guidance Counsellor and the extent to which staff working in guidance and pastoral care
areas co-ordinated and planned their work. Schools did vary widely,
however, in the nature of their personal/social support structures for their
students and in the extent to which school staff, or even specialised
counsellors, engaged in student counselling. While some schools/
Guidance Counsellors did see their role as offering such a service to students, for the most part schools saw themselves in the role of identification and referral of students in need of specialised support. However,
schools were critical of the adequacy and responsiveness of such external
support services and many felt that this was an area which needed urgent
attention.

While most Guidance Counsellors spoke positively of their in-
service training experiences, they were somewhat critical of the extent to
which they were supported in pursuing additional and specialised training and argued for the introduction of financial support to enable them to
enhance their skills and qualifications.

Chapter Seven

GUIDANCE IN SCHOOLS: VARIATIONS ACROSS SCHOOLS AND SOME COMMON ISSUES

7.1 INTRODUCTION

Variation in the nature of school guidance provision was a fundamental finding from both the national survey data and case study analysis. Given the discretionary nature of guidance services and the reluctance of policymakers to clearly prescribe the "guidance role", it is not surprising that the nature, timing and function of guidance services varies widely across schools, as do the experiences of students. The first part of this chapter discusses some of these differences and highlights implications for service delivery and students' guidance experiences. The second part of the chapter draws out some of the central and common issues facing the second-level guidance services today. Drawing on qualitative data derived from evaluations of the guidance services by personnel working in the schools, the discussion considers the key strengths, weaknesses and priorities for the future development of guidance.

7.2 VARIATION ACROSS SCHOOLS

7.2.1 Guidance resources

Virtually all schools argued for the need for additional resources and reported that their current time allocation for guidance is not sufficient for their guidance related activities. Some important variations are apparent however, the most notable being disparity between GEI and non-GEI schools, hardly surprising given the boosting of guidance resources in GEI schools. In particular, Guidance Counsellors in schools that were participating in the GEI were more positive about being able to address guidance issues within the allocated time.

Some other important differences emerge: Principals of vocational schools were more likely to feel that students are missing out on guidance; Guidance Counsellors in designated disadvantaged schools were less likely to feel that there are sufficient resources for the Guidance Counsellor's work; while those in very small schools (less than 250 students) were more likely to have concerns over all students accessing guidance and counselling services when necessary.

Within the case study schools, resources allocated to guidance varied considerably. Contrary to work by the NCGE (2001), all schools utilised their departmental guidance allocation (except one school which took three hours from guidance to offer an additional language). However, variation in resource allocation (per capita) resulted from six of the schools adding to their guidance allocation – in some cases utilising funds from their teaching allocation, in others using resources from the School Completion Programme or Special Needs services. Two schools also received additional resources from the GEI.

Hence, while the Department of Education and Science operate a strict quota system for the allocation of guidance resources to schools (with the addition of supplementary resources through the GEI), this by no means ensures equal guidance provision in all schools, with some measure of school management judgement playing a role in the level of guidance service actually operating in a school. In addition, the extent to which a school receives additional discretionary resources (through programmes like the School Completion Programme or voluntary subscriptions) appears to have an impact on the level of guidance provision in a school; having particular implications for schools without access to such discretionary funds.

7.2.2 Need to combine teaching and guidance duties

Chapter Six illustrated some important tensions faced by Guidance Counsellors in juggling their guidance duties and regular teaching work.

Quantitative and qualitative analysis reveals some important differences between schools in the level of teaching "burden" being placed on Guidance Counsellors. Given the quota system for allocating guidance resources to schools, it is not surprising to find a clear relationship between school size and whether a Guidance Counsellor has teaching duties. There were no significant differences between school types, fee-paying status or designated disadvantaged status in teaching responsibilities for Guidance Counsellors. However, those not taking part in the GEI were significantly more likely to have teaching commitments than those in the GEI.

7.2.3 Guidance Counsellor credentials

While the majority of Guidance Counsellors described themselves as qualified Guidance Counsellors, there were significant differences between types of schools in whether the Guidance Counsellor was qualified. While all community/comprehensive school Guidance Counsellors were qualified, qualification levels were somewhat lower in the secondary and vocational sectors. Given the greater reliance on part-time guidance staff in smaller schools, it was not surprising to find fewer qualified staff in such smaller schools.

There was also some variation across schools in the ability of guidance staff to participate in in-service training: Guidance Counsellors in vocational schools and smaller schools were less likely to have received any guidance-related training in the previous year. While there were no major differences across schools in the extent to which Guidance Counsellors found it easy to participate in available guidance-related training, those with teaching commitments did find it more difficult to find time to attend courses.

7.2.4 Approach and role of Guidance Counsellor

Findings from the survey data (Chapters Two and Three) suggest variations in the main activities of Guidance Counsellors across schools differentiated according to school type, gender and designated disadvantaged status, as well as participation in the GEI. Guidance Counsellors in GEI schools are more likely to be involved in personal support/

counselling than those in non-GEI schools, as are Guidance Counsellors operating in designated disadvantaged schools. The role played by Guidance Counsellors in subject choice advice also varied widely, although such variation at junior cycle largely reflected the timing of subject choice.

There was some evidence that guidance duties also reflected, to some extent, the student population they served. Guidance Counsellors' responsibilities relating to students' work experience, for example, varied across schools. Most notably, Guidance Counsellors in designated disadvantaged schools were more likely to rate dealing with work experience as an important activity, a pattern relating to the greater number of vocationally oriented programmes involving work experience in these schools.

The balance of time spent on academic guidance, career guidance and personal guidance also showed some variation across schools. Most notably, Guidance Counsellors in community/comprehensive schools tended to spend somewhat less time on academic guidance and more time on personal guidance than those in secondary or vocational schools. Furthermore, Guidance Counsellors in designated disadvantaged schools spent significantly less time on careers guidance and more time on personal guidance, while Guidance Counsellors in GEI schools also report spending more time on personal guidance. In many ways, designated disadvantaged schools are more likely to take a more holistic and broad conception of guidance.

7.2.5 Nature of personal support/counselling services

Virtually all case study schools argued for the need for greater counselling provision for students, with little differentiation across school types/gender. There was, however, little consensus over the form such additional support should take: within school or outside, school staff or specialised professionals etc. The case study schools captured a range of counselling provision models ranging from highly specialised, to semi-structured, ad hoc to the absence of such supports. Among the models were:

1. Highly structured counselling with specialised counsellors employed by the school;

2. Guidance Counsellors with specialised qualifications offering a one-to-one counselling service to their students;

3. Ad hoc "counselling" arrangements offered by a range of school personnel;

4. The referral of students who presented with personal issues to external agencies;

5. A more narrowly defined Guidance Counsellor role seen as serving the career guidance needs of students and not encompassing counselling.

Where personnel were most satisfied with the social/personal supports for students, they had developed good contacts and a network of contact persons in various external support services – public and private – such as NEPS, social services, private counselling services and other agencies such as Barnardos, the Rape Crisis Centre, Crisis Pregnancy Agency and the Lucena Clinic. In addition, the provision of some in-school professional counselling services was seen to be effective in supporting students and students themselves indicated that they would prefer to approach a non-teaching staff member with a personal problem.

Regardless of the approach taken and the supports operating, the majority of schools argued for the important role they (can) play in the identification and referral of students in need, thereby taking a more proactive preventative approach. In some cases, Guidance Counsellors did feel they had the skills (and training) to take a more central role in the counselling of students. In others, they felt such a role was not appropriate or within their skills/remit. Finally, a number of Guidance Counsellors expressed a desire to offer a more comprehensive counselling service to their students but felt they were inhibited from doing so either by school management views of their role or the lack of financial assistance to undertake the necessary specialised training. In any case, findings suggest varying conceptions of, and attitudes towards, "counselling" in second-level schools. While the benefits of a flexible and loosely defined guidance service allow such a differentiated structure of student support to exist, there is clearly an issue over whether, within such a differentiated setup, all students in need of specialist support and counselling are being identified and referred for the necessary assistance, an issue which would seem particularly pertinent in the context of reports of rising levels of personal and social distress and difficulty among young people, manifested for example in the rising incidence of suicide.

7.2.6 Contact with different year groups

Department of Education and Science Guidelines for Guidance (2005) recommend a balance in guidance provision across junior and senior cycle groups. There was little evidence of such a balanced approach in either the national survey data or the case study analysis. Just two of the case study schools spent any significant guidance time with junior cycle groups (one of which was a GEI school and the other fee-paying). Findings from the national survey, however, indicated some important variations across schools with girls' secondary schools more likely to report timetabled classes with junior cycle students. Similarly, NCGE Audit data (2001) revealed Guidance Counsellors were less likely to spent time with junior cycle classes in vocational schools.

The extent to which a Guidance Counsellor worked with junior cycle groups to a large extent mirrored the level of guidance resources allocated to a school: Guidance Counsellors in larger schools, GEI schools and schools designated disadvantaged were all more likely to spend time with first year students, with similar patterns emerging for time with Junior Certificate students.

7.2.7 Whole school approach/status of guidance

Case study analysis indicated a dichotomy between schools which were successfully taking a more whole school approach to guidance and those where views were more negative about the extent of teacher and wider staff involvement in the guidance/ support areas. In some of these latter schools, there were some concerns over the wider school value placed on guidance, the status of guidance in the school and a lack of awareness of the role of the Guidance Counsellor. In others, the lack of a team approach was argued to be simply due to the lack of time and opportunity to meet. Regardless of whether the school currently operated a co-ordinated and team-based approach to guidance, the majority of key personnel saw it as an important component of an effective and consistent guidance and student support system in a school. Departmental guidelines emphasise the importance of viewing guidance as a whole school responsibility; they note that, while the Guidance Counsellor has primary responsibility for the delivery of the school's guidance and counselling programme, other members of staff have important and worthwhile contributions to make to the planning and delivery of many aspects of guidance and pastoral provision.

Findings from the quantitative analysis again reveal differences between GEI and non-GEI schools – in particular, Guidance Counsellors in GEI schools were considerably more likely to consider all staff aware of how to identify young people in need of specialist advice. An important difference across school types also emerged. Those in boys' secondary schools were more than twice as likely as those in other school types to consider that there is insufficient appreciation of the importance of guidance and counselling among school staff. This raises issues over the value placed on "softer" curricular areas such as guidance within schools serving boys and whether such students are benefiting from the same level of school support as their girls' school counterparts.

7.2.8 External links and supports

Again partly reflecting differing student populations and varying need to draw on more specialised external support, contact with support services such as NEPS, NEWB and other services showed some differentiation across schools. Schools designated disadvantaged and GEI schools were more likely to liaise with external services such as NEPS, NEWB, Youthreach, youth-workers and Juvenile Liaison Officers/Gardaí. Interestingly, vocational schools were less likely to liaise with the NEPS and NEWB compared to other types of schools.

7.2.9 Satisfaction with guidance

While school personnel were generally more satisfied with the vocational and career guidance services they offered than with the personal/ social support services, some important differences did emerge between schools. Those taking part in the GEI were on average more satisfied with the personal/social guidance and counselling and the input into pastoral care for students in their school, as well as with the more general support structures for students in their schools.

Those in vocational schools were less satisfied with academic guidance, as were personnel in small schools (less than 250 students). Principals in secondary schools were more likely to feel their students had a good idea how to apply for college compared to both vocational schools and community schools. Conversely, designated disadvantaged schools were more likely to indicate that students have low aspirations when it comes to thinking about their future. Such designated disadvantaged schools were, however, more satisfied with personal guidance in their schools and were more satisfied with the advice they were offering individual students.

7.2.10 Summary: Differences across schools

This section has revealed important variations across schools in the nature and level of guidance services, with important implications for the guidance experiences of students across schools. Such variations relate to the level of resources for guidance, the qualifications and training of Guidance Counsellors, the role and focus of Guidance Counsellors, the time spent with different year groups, the status of guidance in schools, the role of schools in offering personal/social counselling to students, the links with external support services and satisfaction with guidance services.

In-depth interviews with key personnel in the case study schools allowed some reflection on what staff considered to be the key strengths, weaknesses and priorities for the future development of guidance and support services in their schools. The following sections synthesise some of the more prominent issues that emerged.

7.3 COMMON ISSUES: STRENGTHS OF GUIDANCE AND SUPPORT SERVICES FOR STUDENTS

This section commences with an examination of some of the key strengths emerging in evaluations of guidance and support services for students, as judged by key school personnel. The section reviews two central areas emerging across the schools:

- Human resources

- Career guidance and preparation.

7.3.1 Human Resources

Virtually all of the 15 case-study schools placed strong emphasis on the dedication and hard work of their Guidance Counsellors and teachers performing guidance duties in enabling the provision of comprehensive guidance services to their students. Despite strong concerns over the level of resources devoted to this sector (as discussed below), many of the schools cited the key role played by their Guidance Counsellors in students' lives and decisions and the fact that this role was often under-taken outside of the regular school hours and often at the voluntary initiative of the Guidance Counsellor. Several schools alluded to such dedication in the work of Guidance Counsellors, as illustrated in the following remark:

> Because she gives so much time over her allocated time it's strong [the guidance service]. If she was somebody who came along and said nine hours cut-off, it wouldn't work. It's her ability, her initiative. (Principal, Ashfield Park).

Some of the praise of Guidance Counsellors' work related to their relationships with students, both in terms of their approachability and accessibility/open door policies in a number of schools. In one school, this was reflected in the level of demand by students to see her.

> She is absolutely snowed under all the time, people want to make appointments and talk to her, which I think is a real indication that the job is being well done. (Deputy Principal, Whitefield).

In many schools, the fact that such a key support person is easily accessed by students is seen as a vital part of student life and an integral part of the Guidance Counsellor's role.

> The main strengths are students now have somebody who can take them aside for 40 minutes and give them 100 per cent attention. That is the main strength. I feel students show huge emotion when they realise somebody is actually listening. (Guidance Counsellor, Rosendale).

> . . . availability of the person [GC], provision for every child to be treated equally and no one to say well she will only see or only has time for . . . you often hear this, people might only spend time with high flyers. (Guidance Counsellor, Ashfield Park).

7.3.2 Career guidance and preparation

In the vast majority of the case study schools, key personnel were broadly satisfied with the career guidance students were receiving, and a number of the schools considered this area the main strength in evaluating their guidance services. Such guidance largely related to the areas of CAO advice, advice regarding what colleges and courses to pursue and advice regarding post-school educational options.

> The main strength . . . is that the students are provided with the information they need to make decisions. And they are supported in making those decisions and the parents are kept involved. (Guidance Counsellor, Riverbank).

> I would certainly see the main strengths as being the vocational guidance . . . because there's such a gap of knowledge among parents and guardians about the opportunities that are available for people in terms of third level education, in terms of going into college, in terms of careers or in terms of student needs, that is hugely important that there is some pointers available for them. (Guidance Counsellor, Lawton Way).

In many ways, this reflects the predominant focus on "careers" across almost all of the case study schools, particularly career guidance for fifth and sixth year groups. This appears to reflect a priority given to careers within a very limited time allowance, as well as reflecting the demands of students, and parents, for such guidance.

> Well my main responsibility is to ensure everybody gets proper career information . . . that is quite important to the school and to the parents. That they would be able to face the Leaving Cert, CAO and changing to third level. (Guidance Counsellor, Riverbank).

> Primarily I am in a one-to-one role facilitating students doing research on careers. I'm really addressing any questions, issues, helping them with paper work with the CAO and so forth. (Guidance Counsellor, Cherryfield View).

In many schools, this focus on "careers" and a "culture of careers" is seen as having a positive impact on students' career preparation. School personnel had largely positive views of both students' level of preparedness for progressing to further education after school and the rate of progression to further and higher education. First, many of the schools expressed satisfaction with the rate of progression to further study:

> I don't have the statistics but the vast majority would go on to further studies. (Principal, Chestnut Drive).

> Traditionally we had a good rate of students going to all faculties and colleges. (Guidance Counsellor, Riverbank).

Second, the majority felt that students were also academically well prepared for progressing to further study.

> I would think that the students are very well prepared for getting into whatever course they choose to get into. (Deputy Principal, Whitefield).

> The colleges are always very pleased and very willing to send down people to promote their college and to talk about them and very often they say about how well prepared students have been that they have got in from here. (Principal, Greenwood).

However, a number of schools alluded to the different learning styles between second and third level systems and the difficulties this created for students, an issue which is discussed further below.

7.4 WEAKNESSES OF GUIDANCE AND SUPPORT SERVICES FOR STUDENTS

Again deriving from interviews with key personnel across the case study schools, a number of areas of weakness were prominent in evaluating the guidance services in their school. These included:

- Resources

- External support structures

- Inadequate guidance at junior cycle

- Student preparedness on a personal/social level.

7.4.1 Resources

Just two of the 15 case study schools expressed any sense of satisfaction with the level of resources for Guidance.

> Interviewer: Do you think the school has sufficient resources for guidance and counselling?

> Principal: I never like saying I have sufficient of anything because it's so unlike me, the department would be really shocked if they thought I was saying that. You see from the point of view of guidance at the moment I think yes [we have sufficient resources]. (Cherryfield View).

In each of the other schools, concerns around the level of resources were expressed, sometimes on quite a strongly worded basis.

> Certainly as Principal when I make an application for resources just to get blanket no is, I find it discouraging. (Principal, Riverbank).

There was also strong criticism of the system of allocation of resources and the inflexibility of the quota system. Some schools expressed dissatisfaction with the need to draw on resources from other sources to fulfil guidance needs.

Ultimately, the shortcomings in resources were invariably reflected in the time allocation for Guidance:

Interviewer: What is the main weakness with the guidance services in your school?

Principal: Simply a lack of time for the whole area of guidance. (Oakhill Way).

While a strong focus on careers and vocational guidance was seen as a key strength in many of the schools, the corollary of this is a perceived neglect of the more student support/counselling aspect of the Guidance Counsellor's role. With limitations in time and resources, many schools and Guidance Counsellors felt they were unable to offer an adequate personal support and counselling role to their students.

In line with a perceived short-fall in guidance resources, some personnel also maintained that there was insufficient time for planning and interaction among staff regarding guidance and counselling issues. Others pointed to the difficulties in balancing a guidance role with that of a teaching role and argued for the need for a full-time guidance allocation in all schools.

7.4.2 External support structures

As discussed in Chapter Six, many schools drew attention to inadequacies in the supports offered to schools, particularly relating to the services of NEPS and the health boards/social services.

Many of the concerns related to the level of financial support available to the support services. In relation to the operations of the NEPS, there were widespread concerns over the lack of funding and the consequently lengthy waiting lists and lack of response to perceived needs.

I would like to see more easier access to outside services. Like psychological services. They are ferociously stretched in the Department of Education. (Principal, Hills Road).

Similar concerns related to the support offered by the social services and particularly their level of resources.

I think what is frustrating for a lot of people is the lack of response. . . . Social workers do their best, I wouldn't criticise them, I know the psychiatric services are overburdened, people will put them on waiting lists, they mightn't be seen for months. I know I had a situation a

> few years ago where a child was in desperate need of . . . special counselling and she was put on the waiting list and for the duration of the two years she was here she never got counselling. (Guidance Counsellor, Ashfield Park).

Some key personnel also expressed a great difficulty in accessing and identifying the relevant personnel in the support services.

> I would like an improvement on the existing services and for them to be more visible. I would like them to network with us, make contact with us, let us know who they are, where they are, how we contact them. And even to establish some kind of relationship with them. (Guidance Counsellor, Maplewood).

The issue of resource allocation and the perceived inflexibility of the system of allocation of resources also emerged and schools which were faced with the need for urgent counselling services felt they were then penalised in their allocation of time for assessments.

As noted earlier, given the difficulties in accessing such support services, many of the schools indicated students and schools were being forced to rely on private provision, particularly in the area of counselling.

> In recent times now the psychological services have come in, we have had tests and they give recommendations. But the reality is that some kids unless they can pay won't be able to get it. And the vast majority of parents can't pay. (Principal, Rosendale).

7.4.3 Inadequate guidance at junior cycle

With the exception of one of the GEI schools (which was using the additional resources to offer guidance services at junior cycle), virtually all of the case study schools expressed concern over the level of guidance being offered to junior cycle students. This has important implications for subject and programme choice at senior cycle, as well as developing more general abilities such as decision-making skills and the ability to source information, as well as identifying areas of interest at an earlier age.

I think that the Junior Certs should be introduced to career guidance and I think there should be a greater understanding of what career guidance is for students. (Guidance Counsellor, Willow Grove).

[If given additional resources] I would begin by providing service to third year; there is a major deficiency there. (Principal, Willow Grove).

If I had the time I'd like to be more involved with the junior cycle but I just feel that if I try to do that in a big way other areas of the senior cycle would suffer. (Guidance Counsellor, Lawton Way).

7.4.4 Student preparedness on personal/social level

Interviews also examined the views of staff on the extent to which they felt students were prepared for leaving school: in terms of academic, personal and social preparedness. In many of the interviews, issues around the personal and social maturity of students emerged, as well as concerns over the different teaching and learning styles typically operating at second and third level.

Interviewer: Are there any areas where you feel students might be better prepared?

Deputy Principal: I suppose the non-academic; we have pushed them to the Leaving. . . . That is a huge need, a social preparation. (Chestnut Drive).

Many comments related to the social and emotional maturity of students and the extent to which they had the skills to enter into more independent living arrangements.

Interviewer: Are there any areas where you feel students might be better prepared?

Principal: I suppose the area of acting independently, you know. That they can live without the vigilance of their teachers. Like that you are operating on other people's responsibility rather than your own, we could work on that. I suppose just life coping skills . . . you know we could be doing more in the area of self esteem and independent thinking. (Chestnut Drive).

I think they could be better prepared and I think it's a criticism of all schools. There is probably too much school time when they are in the secondary system with the result that some of them find the freedom of third level that they can't cope. Because they have been so supervised and monitored and advised at second level that some of them certainly can't cope with third level and the freedom they have there. (Principal, Oakhill Way).

The change in learning style from teacher-directed to more self-directed learning in third level was seen as an important issue which faced students progressing to third level and one which schools were not addressing.

Interviewer: Are there any areas where you feel students might be better prepared?

Guidance Counsellor: Maybe better to study on their own without, the secondary system has a lot of teacher input, maybe an old fashioned word of spoon feeding and I find when they move away from that even with my own children they found that difficult. So maybe more responsibility for their own study at school. Maybe more responsibility in the system. (Beechwood Square).

So there is no emphasis on the self learning. That is a huge shock when they get to college. . . . The emphasis would have to be taken from the directed learning. It's more personal development than just sitting down at a desk and absorbing the stuff. Their critical thinking skills aren't there. (Beechwood Square).

However, schools varied in their perceptions of students' maturity and personal/social readiness for leaving school. A number of schools identified the availability of the Transition Year programme as a key determinant of such readiness:

The Transition Year makes a huge difference, they are more mature . . . but Transition Year the difference is extraordinary . . . they are more rooted in where they are going. (Guidance Counsellor, Whitefield).

I find the pupils who have come through the Transition Year much more focused and seem to have more coping skills. . . . Perhaps because they are a year older, perhaps they have had an experience to develop themselves somewhat in the Transition Year programme through interacting with each other and maybe at a different level with the teachers. (Guidance Counsellor, Beechwood Square).

Differences between Leaving Certificate Applied and regular Leaving Certificate students were also noted in a number of schools; with personnel maintaining that LCVP and, more particularly, LCA students had a greater sense of initiative and an ability to think independently, had greater inter-personal skills and were better prepared for the labour market.

> The LCA prepares them a bit better for work, they do work experience one day a week . . . they would be better prepared for life afterwards. (Seaview).

> Interviewer: Would you say there is a variation between the Leaving Cert Applied and regular Leaving Cert groups?

> Principal: The LCA group is far more prepared for the interview situation, interacting with adults, knowledge of the work place. They would be interacting with managerial people within the work place, they would definitely be far better prepared, that would be very much part of the process they go through as part of the course. Whereas, the LCE would be more book focused, study focused and the ability to develop those interpersonal skills to a degree falls short because of the academic element. (Cherryfield View).

Where schools felt students were socially and emotionally prepared for leaving school, it appears programmes such as the Transition Year and Leaving Certificate Applied played a central role in such preparation. An emphasis on preparedness did not appear to occupy a more general position in the schools, but rather was an area that many schools felt was largely neglected.

7.5 PRIORITIES FOR THE FUTURE

7.5.1 Resources

Almost all schools expressed a need for additional resources for guidance and counselling.

> I think every school should be allocated a full guidance teacher regardless of the size. (Principal, Cherryfield View).

> Allocate more career Guidance Counsellors. More people to the area,
> I think years and years ago there was one allocation per one hundred
> and fifty [students] (*sic*), which we would need three then at that
> rate. And at a time when counselling is just as important, the need
> for counselling would not have been anything like it is now. (Deputy
> Principal, Whitefield).

A number suggested that there should be greater targeting of additional
resources in favour of certain schools, particularly schools located in
more economically disadvantaged areas.

> I firmly believe that schools that are deemed disadvantaged we need a
> full-time Guidance Counsellor outside of the allocation. Purely to give
> all of the kids access, they all need access. (Principal, Rosendale).

> On a national level the big difficulty that I see happening in terms of
> guidance . . . is people are inclined to feel that if any initiative that
> comes out it has to be mainstreamed, in other words you can't have a
> Guidance Counsellor all to yourself because everybody will want
> one. . . . I think there should be some positive discrimination . . . in
> favour of schools that have proven that because of their location and
> so on that there are greater needs within them. (Principal, Lawton
> Way).

7.5.2 Greater focus on junior cycle

The issue of guidance at junior cycle and the difficulties schools encountered in finding time or resources to offer such guidance emerged frequently. There was also a recognition in many of the case study schools
that such earlier guidance needs to be more adequately developed in future guidance services.

> That you would target the junior school in career guidance. And that
> a programme would be put in place that a child would be aware from
> first year on that decisions are going to be made about her life even if
> she doesn't make them but she is aware of the consequences of sub-
> ject choices. (Deputy Principal, Beechwood Square).

> If I got additional resources . . . targeting the first and second years
> for subject choice and skills, working to schedules, that type of thing.
> (Deputy Principal, Rosendale).

My vision would be that they come in in first year and we have regular meetings with them and they know the child and the parents. Where the child wants to go. So that you are not only getting to them in fifth year. (Principal, Ashfield Park).

7.5.3 Greater provision of counselling/personal support for students

As discussed in Chapter Four, the case study schools varied widely in the role played in personal/social support and counselling for students and in the staffing and resources targeted at this area. A number of schools employed trained psychotherapists to visit the school on a regular basis to counsel students; others availed of third level counselling students who sought work placements; while others referred all students perceived to be in need of such support to outside state or private services.

A large number of the case study schools did express a need for further attention in this area and an issue which the schools needed to address more adequately in the future.

If I got additional resources, the counselling side. Counselling for students. (Deputy Principal, Rosendale).

This was seen as a particular need for those schools that did not have a Chaplain position.

But allied to greater provision of counselling/personal support for students, a number of Guidance Counsellors commented on the need for supervision and comprehensive training to fulfil this role professionally.

Across all schools, however, there was a view that, if schools are to play a central role in the identification of students experiencing difficulties and their referral to specialist supports where necessary, comprehensive and responsive external support services must be available.

7.6 SUMMARY AND DISCUSSION

This Chapter details some important variations across schools in the nature and level of guidance services for students. Such variations partly relate to resources and the availability of additional (GEI) and discretionary resources, with implications for the level and breadth of guidance provision across schools as well as the availability of guidance for different, particularly junior cycle, year groups. More generally, there are important variations in the qualifications of Guidance Counsellors and their ability to pursue in-service training, in the role and activities of Guidance Counsellors, in their links with external support services and in school personnel, and student, satisfaction with guidance.

The analysis also raises some important central issues regarding the guidance services operating in second-level schools. There is widespread satisfaction with the level of commitment and dedication of Guidance Counsellors. However, this does raise issues over success being contingent on the commitment and personality of the Guidance Counsellor. This is particularly important in the context of serious concerns over the level of resourcing of guidance services and the difficulties this is creating on the ground. Such difficulties are reflected in the time allowed for guidance activities, the extent to which this allows adequate guidance across all year groups and comprehensiveness in terms of a broad career and counselling remit. Also the difficulties in combining teaching and guidance roles are noted.

The second main issue emerging is the focus of guidance services and school ethos more generally. In many schools, owing partly to student and parent demand, guidance is largely confined to career preparation and progression to further study. More general issues of social and emotional preparedness for life beyond school are largely neglected and any work that is done in this area is related to participation in programmes such as Transition Year and the Leaving Certificate Applied, rather than being a more central aspect of guidance and support services, and indeed the wider curriculum, in schools.

Chapter Eight

SUMMARY AND RECOMMENDATIONS

8.1 INTRODUCTION

This study has comprehensively considered the function and operation of
guidance services in second-level schools from the perspectives of key
school personnel and students alike. The study has placed particular emphasis on the diverse and varying roles of Guidance Counsellors in Irish
schools and defined guidance in its broad terms of career guidance and
social/personal counselling. In so doing, the study recognises the importance of career guidance for the development of human capital. As work
on human capital (OCED, 2002) suggests, career management skills may
play an important role in economic growth: people's ability to build, and
to manage, their skills, including career-planning, job-search and other
career-management skills are of great importance. In addition, however,
the study equally considers the nature and effects of personal and social
supports and pastoral care arrangements in schools. Such supports are
seen to play a central role in addressing the social and personal concerns
of students and as such contribute to the broader social-psychological
development of young people.

This chapter summarises some of the key findings emerging from the
study and identifies various recommendations for policy.

8.2 SUMMARY OF MAIN FINDINGS

A review of policy documents on guidance services revealed a certain
ambiguity over the structure and nature of guidance in second-level
schools. While to some extent this has reflected a resistance against too
much role definition on the part of Guidance Counsellors, particularly in

the early days of the guidance service, it has also arisen from a lack of an overall policy framework for guidance. Guidelines for schools on the implications of the Education Act (1998) for guidance were circulated (for consultation) in September 2003, followed by the publication of the document in 2005. However, there is still no clear overall policy statement on guidance. Aside from standard criteria for the allocation of guidance resources (through the quota system based on pupil enrolment), there is no clear standardised framework for guidance services in second-level schools.

Arising from such a policy context, Guidance Counsellors play varying roles across schools. Such variations also reflect diverging views on the most effective and appropriate role, and indeed skills, of Guidance Counsellors, variations in guidance resources, variations in student needs and parental demands/expectations and differences across schools in the extent of a whole school or team-based approach to guidance and student support. As a result, the nature and content of guidance services varies across schools and different year groups. While some schools offer broad career guidance, academic guidance and personal and social support to all students, others define guidance more narrowly in terms of careers and academic guidance, with such guidance often targeted at senior cycle students.

Schools are critical of the level of resources allocated to guidance services and express great difficulty in offering a comprehensive guidance service to their students with such limited resources. The vast majority of Guidance Counsellors feel that some students are missing out on the guidance and counselling they need. Nearly all Guidance Counsellors also found their current time allocation insufficient for their guidance-related activities. Schools in the position to draw on discretionary funds (particularly schools designated disadvantaged), such as through programmes like the School Completion Programme or through voluntary subscriptions, or benefiting from participation in the GEI, are often in a position to offer a more comprehensive guidance service. Indeed, larger schools (benefiting from a greater guidance allocation) are also more likely to offer a comprehensive guidance service – that is, one addressing the social and personal counselling needs of students, as well as a guidance programme targeting junior as well as senior cycle students. Having increased resources for guidance appears to facilitate greater involvement in general academic support, personal support and assisting students with special needs, that is, a broader range of activities beyond a narrow focus on career guidance.

Schools participating in the GEI spoke positively of their experiences and noted the impact the Initiative has had on the guidance services in their schools. Indeed, findings from the national survey indicate that the additional resources enable these schools to broaden their focus beyond career guidance towards a greater emphasis on personal support and counselling. In addition, such schools also place greater focus on students in the junior cycle, a focus which can be seen to play an important role in ensuring informed subject and programme choices among students.

The issue of junior cycle guidance more generally emerged in case study and national survey data; in particular, schools and students varied widely in their perceptions and experiences of such guidance. As noted above, schools with greater resources have greater involvement with junior cycle groups, particularly GEI and larger schools. Some students were critical of the guidance they received during their junior cycle years and noted the implications this had for their subject, programme and post-school choices and the limitations imposed by uninformed choices during the junior and senior cycle years; a concern that was also noted in a recent study by Forfás (2006). Given that some students leave school early, the implications of inadequate, or indeed an absence of, junior cycle guidance are also important for these students. How are such early leavers to make informed choices about their post-school options if they have had little exposure to guidance? Guidance should play a central role in making such students aware of the implications of such early school leaving for their educational and labour market opportunities.

While the majority of schools were broadly satisfied with the level and nature of career guidance offered to senior cycle students in their schools, such guidance was often narrowly framed in terms of post-school third level choices and CAO applications. There appeared to be a relative neglect of non-third level educational and training opportunities, such as Post Leaving Certificate courses, training courses and apprenticeships. In addition, there was little evidence that guidance was promoting non-traditional subject and career choice. Students themselves would have liked more information and advice on post-school options, particularly outside of the CAO system and non-mainstream courses and careers. This raises important issues concerning the educational and labour market choices of young people and the extent to which non-mainstream, non-gender stereotyped and alternative educational routes are promoted in schools.

Many Guidance Counsellors face the situation of juggling subject teaching with their guidance responsibilities. In a context of limited resources, many found such juggling difficult and it impinged on their capacity to deliver a comprehensive guidance service to their students. Such a dual role was also perceived as making it difficult to promote a caring, supportive, non-disciplinarian image to their students. More generally, such a dual role created ambiguity over the professional status of Guidance Counsellors and their status in schools more generally. While some were viewed as part of a separate professional body within their schools, others faced a tension with fellow workers over their status and professional identity.

Overall, there was a lack of guidance planning across schools, with members of staff finding it difficult to find time to meet. Schools which had completed written guidance plans, as required to, reported greater satisfaction with personal guidance, academic guidance and careers guidance, probably reflecting a greater whole school commitment to guidance in these schools.

Guidance Counsellors spoke positively about their experiences of in-service training, often for the opportunities such training allowed to meet with other guidance counsellors. However, there were issues over teachers with guidance hours being allowed time to attend such training, particularly in smaller schools. In addition, guidance staff more generally were critical of the level of financial support available to undertake advanced and specialised training in their field.

8.3 RECOMMENDATIONS

While this book details broad and wide-ranging aspects of guidance counselling services within second-level schools, and indeed external statutory and private supports beyond the school setting, a number of key areas can be identified for further policy attention:

1. Departmental policy on guidance counselling services

2. School autonomy versus standardised provision

3. Resources

4. Whole school approach to guidance and school guidance plans

5. Addressing the career guidance needs of all students

6. Addressing the personal/social counselling needs of all students

7. Junior cycle guidance

8. Incorporating parents into guidance.

8.3.1 Departmental level policy and guidelines

Policy on guidance services varies widely across European countries, in line with wide variations in the nature, provision and function of guidance services. Irish policy on guidance services has been somewhat fragmented and *ad hoc* with no overall policy governing the provision of guidance services in second-level schools. While a number of key education policy documents (such as the Green Paper on Education, Education Act, 1998) refer to guidance, there is no comprehensive policy dealing with the issue. The Education Act, for example, refers to the need for "appropriate guidance" for all students although no attempt is made to specify how the services should actually operate or be delivered in schools.

The lack of overall policy on guidance in Irish schools to some extent stems from the nature and historical development of the guidance service. For example, no attempt has been made by policymakers to define the role of the Guidance Counsellor, at second level or any other level of education. There is a lack of clear definition in relation to guidance counselling at the policy level. Any definitions that have emerged have tended to be general in nature and often developed by the NCGE or IGC, rather than the Department of Education and Science. Such role definitions frequently tend to present a wide range of activities or duties

of the Guidance Counsellor, with little consideration of the relative importance of each of these tasks or the priority to be accorded to each. There
has also been no attempt to ensure universal guidance functions. The result
is wide variation in the nature of guidance services and personal/social
supports being experienced by students. While some students receive early
and comprehensive career guidance advice facilitating informed subject,
programme and career choices, others have more limited exposure to these
services.

While the current report welcomes the recent availability of "Guidelines for Second-Level Schools on the implications of Section 9 (C) of
the Education Act (1998), relating to students' access to appropriate
guidance" (2005), there is a need for a more comprehensive policy on
guidance services in second-level schools.

8.3.2 School autonomy versus standardised provision

One of the strengths of the guidance services at second level is the ability
of schools to respond flexibly to individual needs and to allow sensitivity
to different school contexts, with schools to a large extent determining
the exact nature and role of their guidance services. Some schools place
predominant focus on the career preparation of their students, often narrowly defined in terms of third level/CAO preparation, while others see
their guidance services as fulfilling the broader function of the personal
and social support of students as well as career guidance. While such a
largely "discretionary" system ensures flexibility and the opportunity for
schools to respond to particular needs, it does also create a situation in
which students in some schools are receiving a vastly different guidance
and support system to students in other schools. Ideally, students should
have the right to make informed choices both early during junior cycle in
relation to subjects and programmes, for example, and at senior cycle
with regard to post-school career decisions. On this basis, the report recommends that all students should receive a core set of key guidance information, covering subject (level) choice, (senior cycle) programme
choice, exam preparation and study skills and career preparation. Such a
standard career guidance component could be delivered either through a
guidance module for each year group, or at the very least first, third,

Transition Year, fifth and sixth year students, or through the introduction of timetabled guidance classes, perhaps alternating with another subject such as SPHE.

8.3.3 Resources/allocation

Many of the criticisms of the guidance services in second-level schools related to the level of resources allocated to this sector. Schools were highly critical of the level of funding and had serious questions over their capacity to deliver a comprehensive guidance counselling service to all of their students within such a limited budget. Lack of resources manifested in several ways. Many felt the need to concentrate, often solely, on senior cycle students. Others felt they were not in a position to offer an adequate system of personal/social support to their students, but rather felt the need to focus their limited resources on the career preparation of their students. Guidance Counsellors, in particular, were critical of the requirement (for many of them) to juggle subject teaching with their guidance duties and also referred to the conflicts this created between promoting a supportive non-judgemental role in their guidance counselling role and the disciplinary role of teaching.

Schools also varied widely in the actual level of resources they could devote to their guidance services. Some schools were in a position to use discretionary resources from programmes like the School Completion Programme or from their voluntary subscriptions for their guidance counselling services. Across many schools, however, the success of the guidance counselling services was contingent on the goodwill and dedication of the Guidance Counsellor.

Our findings suggest that schools were positive about the GEI and felt it made an important contribution to the provision of a comprehensive guidance service to junior and senior cycle students in their schools. The findings clearly support the continuation of funding to schools currently participating in the GEI. However, the findings also suggest the need for additional funding. While additional resources have been put in place since September 2005, with an increased allocation of guidance hours and a more finely graduated guidance allocation across school sizes, it remains to be seen whether such increased resources adequately address the difficulties faced by schools at the time this research was undertaken.

While the recent resource increases were allocated across all schools based on their size, the current report would agree that there is a strong case for the allocation of any additional funding through the quota system. The GEI targeted designated disadvantaged schools very effectively[11], and was found to have a very positive impact on the nature and effectiveness of the guidance and counselling services in such schools. Designated disadvantaged schools in the case study analysis were found to have considerable guidance resources relative to other schools, partly arising from the allocation of discretionary funds to such schools, such as through the School Completion Programme. On this basis, this report argues that the revisions to the "quota" system of allocation were a positive development. Furthermore, the findings would support the introduction of a minimum guidance allocation of 11 hours and the further boosting of the allocation of guidance resources to schools in the 300-500 enrolment and 600-799 enrolment categories.

Whatever the basis for the allocation of additional resources, a number of conditions should be met before schools are allocated such resources. Most importantly, schools should have developed a comprehensive collaborative (whole school) guidance and counselling policy, identifying areas where need is greatest, in order to receive additional funds. If a targeted approach is to be adopted, schools should demonstrate how they intend to use the resources to address issues of educational underachievement and early school leaving. Also, if a targeted approach is adopted, all (relevant) schools should be made aware of the availability of the additional funding and fully informed about the aims and functions of the additional funds.

The report also recommends that there should be time allocated for teachers with guidance hours, particularly in smaller schools, to allow them to participate in in-service training. The report also identifies a

---

[11] In total 69 per cent of the GEI schools in the national survey (reported in Chapters Two and Three) are designated disadvantaged, relative to 21 per cent of non-GEI schools.

need for schools to be given a greater allocation to undertake whole school planning (as discussed below).

8.3.4 Whole school approach to guidance and school guidance plans

Earlier research (Jeffers, 2002) suggested that Guidance Counsellors often faced a tension between their unique and professional role as Guidance Counsellor and guidance counselling as part of a more collegial and whole school function. The same study goes on to argue that such a separation of duties is in many ways a traditional feature of Irish schools, where individual teachers tend to operate in professional isolation from their colleagues (p. 11). Other research has pointed to a lack of wider staff awareness of the Guidance Counsellor's role: McKenna *et al.* (1997) found that more than a third of Principals described their state of knowledge of guidance and counselling issues as "inadequate".

This study similarly pointed to a lack of awareness of the role of the Guidance Counsellor in many schools and a lack of co-ordination on guidance and pastoral care issues. First, there is a clear need for schools to ensure that all staff are aware of the nature and function of the guidance role. Rather than see it as an isolated role in a school, guidance and the role of the Guidance Counsellor should be seen as part of a wider staff team addressing the career guidance needs of students as well as offering personal and social support. Such an emphasis on a collaborative approach is evident in numerous policy documents: the Green Paper, for example, as well as in NCGE (1996) and IGC (1995) documents, but clearly needs to be promoted within schools.

The study also revealed a widespread lack of guidance planning across schools. While all schools are required to have a written guidance plan in place, clearly this has not yet been completed across many schools. While the NCGE has focused attention on promoting such planning in schools, there is an important need to encourage schools to undertake such planning. This seems particularly important in the context of an association between having a written guidance plan and greater satisfaction with academic guidance, personal guidance and careers guidance. Such guidance planning should be seen as an integral part of whole school planning, with guidance planning being undertaken though collaboration among all staff.

8.3.5 Addressing the career guidance needs of all students

While school personnel were, for the most part, satisfied with the career guidance services they offered to their students, there was an important issue over career guidance largely being narrowly conceived as relating to the process of CAO applications and third level college/course selection. Students, in particular, were critical of the narrow range of course and career options covered. Indeed, an earlier study of third level students (Healy, Carpenter and Lynch, 1999) indicates that non-completion of higher education courses is strongly associated with unclear career aspirations and a lack of information and guidance on course and career options at second level. The study finds that "students who left were especially critical of the type of guidance and information they had received about the academic, organisational and financial demands of their chosen course, prior to entry. Students need greater guidance in making course choices" (p. 4).

There is a clear need to promote a broader definition of career guidance in schools. First, guidance should facilitate non-traditional subject and career choice. A broader definition of guidance should also incorporate non-third level progression routes such as further education courses and PLCs, as well as training courses and apprenticeships. There should be greater visibility and awareness of alternative routes to different occupations and careers, which seems particularly important when students do not attain sufficient "points" or grades to secure their aspired course place. Finally, such comprehensive career guidance provision should also incorporate information on career and further education and training opportunities abroad.

8.3.6 Addressing the personal/social support and counselling needs of students

Recent reports of high levels of social/personal difficulties being experienced by young people, including a high incidence of suicide by international comparison, raise important questions over the nature of the support services operating in second-level schools. This study reveals wide variation in the role of schools and Guidance Counsellors in addressing the personal and social concerns of their students. While to some extent such disparity reflects variations in student need, resources and skills, there was also an important divergence in views regarding the role of schools in offering counselling services to students. While some schools offered an important and valuable specialised counselling service to its students, others did not see such a role as either appropriate or within the remit of the school.

This report would recommend that schools that are offering specialist counselling services to students in need should be facilitated in doing so and adequate resources should be made available to ensure such a service is offered in a professional and competent manner.

The study illustrates the important roles of prevention, identification and appropriate referral for schools in dealing with the personal and social concerns of students. Such a role needs to be seen as not just within the domain of the Guidance Counsellor, but as integrated into wider whole school structures. Schools should be encouraged and facilitated to play an important role in the prevention and identification of students experiencing difficulty. Schools should be offered adequate whole school in-service training on the identification of students in difficulty. Guidance Counsellors should be made fully aware of the nature of support services available and all services should have visible and known personnel to liaise with schools. Perhaps most importantly, the external support services must be adequately funded if they are to offer a comprehensive, responsive and effective service to schools and students in need. Earlier research (NESF, 2002) noted that the NEPS had a difficulty in recruiting staff because of an insufficient number of graduates qualifying in educational psychology to meet current needs; they recommended that more third-level training places should be made available. It appears that difficulties surrounding recruitment persist, alongside inadequate funding of the service, issues which must be addressed if social/personal and educational difficulties being experienced by young people are to be effectively tackled.

8.3.7 Guidance for junior cycle students

A study in the early 1980s (Hannan *et al.,* 1983) identified a serious imbalance in the provision of guidance services at junior and senior cycle
levels: ". . . we found that their (Guidance Counsellor's) role in career
and subject guidance is mainly concentrated at the senior cycle level. . . .
They are much less involved in junior cycle choices" (p. 320). The present study, over 20 years later, reveals a continuation of the imbalance in
favour of senior cycle students.

Such an imbalance has a number of implications relating to inadequate levels of guidance on subject choice and Leaving Certificate programme choice, which in turn makes it difficult to address issues surrounding sex differentiated curricula and pupil choices. Student attitudes
to subject areas and their occupational aspirations appear to be formed at
a relatively early stage. Taking particular subjects for the Junior Certificate is likely to enhance the chances of taking related subjects at senior
cycle level. Furthermore, the variety of jobs students aspire to prior to
the Junior Certificate exam are quite predictive of the kinds of courses
they will take on entry to higher education (Smyth and Hannan, 2002).
Given the importance of early attitudes and aspirations, it is important
that comprehensive information on subjects and careers be provided to
junior cycle students. This may be particularly important for subject areas, such as science, which have experienced declining take-up in recent
years.

In addition, given the predominant focus on senior cycle students in
many schools, those leaving school earlier, i.e. early school leavers, are
found to have had little contact with guidance. As the recent Chief Inspectors Report (2005) noted, the imbalance in the provision of guidance
between senior and junior cycle is of particular concern if pupils at risk
of early school leaving do not have access to appropriate guidance. There
is an urgent need to ensure adequate career guidance for young people at
risk of early school leaving. In particular, such guidance should raise
awareness of the consequences of early school leaving as well as famili-
arity with the range of educational, training and labour market options
open to them.

All schools should be encouraged to ensure a comprehensive career
guidance programme is in place for students throughout junior cycle,

perhaps through a standard guidance component in the junior cycle curriculum.

8.3.8 Incorporating parents into guidance

While Guidance Counsellors play a central role in offering career and educational guidance to young people, findings from the national school leavers' survey indicate that parents play a crucially important role in advising young people on post-school educational and labour market choices. Such a parental role is particularly important among those leaving school prior to Leaving Certificate standard, perhaps partly reflecting the predominant focus of guidance on sixth year students in many schools. In any case, parents play an important role in the career decisions of young people and as such must be incorporated into the guidance programmes in schools. All parents should be made aware of the nature and effects of the educational choices (subjects, subject levels and programmes) their children are making. Schools should be encouraged to involve parents in their guidance programmes, for example, by operating information evenings for parents on guidance issues.

GLOSSARY

JCSP	Junior Certificate School Programme
CEDEFOP	The European Centre for the Development of Vocational Training
GEI	Guidance Enhancement Initiative
IGC	Institute of Guidance Counsellors
LCA	Leaving Certificate Applied
LCVP	Leaving Certificate Vocational Programme
NCGE	National Centre for Guidance in Education
NEPS	National Educational Psychological Service
OECD	Organisation for Economic Cooperation and Development
SPHE	Social, Personal and Health Education
TY	Transition Year

REFERENCES

Coolahan, J. (ed.) (1994). *Report of the National Education Convention*, Dublin: Stationery Office.

Darmody, M. and E. Smyth (2005). *Gender and Subject Choice. Take-up of Technological Subjects in Second-Level Education*, Dublin: Economic and Social Research Institute in association with The Liffey Press.

Department of Education and Science (2003). *"Guidelines for Second Level Schools on the implications of Section 9C of the Education Act (1998), relating to students' access to appropriate guidance"*, Draft for Consultation. Retrieved from http://www.education.ie/servlet/blobservlet/pp_guidance_section_9c.doc

Department of Education and Science (2005). *"Guidelines for Second Level Schools on the implications of Section 9C of the Education Act (1998), relating to students' access to appropriate guidance"*. Retrieved from http://www.education.ie/servlet/blobservlet/pp_guidelines_second_level_schools _9c.pdf?language=EN

Department of Education and Science (2005). *The Chief Inspector's Report 2001-2004*, Dublin: Stationery Office.

Ellis, T.I. (1990). *The Missouri Comprehensive Guidance Model. Highlights: An ERIC/CAPS Digest*. ERIC/CAPS Digests ED315699. Ann Arbor, MI: ERIC, The Educational Resources Information Center.

Eurydice (2005). *Eurybase*, retrieved from http://www.eurydice.org/Eurybase/frameset_eurybase.html

Forfás (2006). *Careers and Labour Market Information in Ireland*, A Study for the Expert Group on Future Skill Needs, Dublin: Forfás.

Government of Ireland (1992). *Education for a Changing World, Green Paper on Education*, Dublin: Stationery Office.

Government of Ireland (1995). *Education for a Changing World, White Paper on Education*, Dublin: Stationery Office.

Government of Ireland (1998). *Education Act 1998*, Dublin: Stationery Office.

Government of Ireland (1999). *The National Development Plan 2000-2006*, Dublin: Stationery Office.

Government of Ireland (2000). *Education Welfare Act*, Dublin: Stationery Office.

Hannan, D.F., R. Breen, B. Murray, D. Watson, N. Hardiman and K. O'Higgins (1983). *Schooling and Sex Roles: Sex Differences in Subject Provision and Student Choice in Irish Post-Primary Schools*, General Research Paper No. 113, Dublin: Economic and Social Research Institute.

Healy, M., A. Carpenter and K. Lynch (1999). *Study of first year students at Institutes of Technology*, Dublin: Dublin Institute of Technology.

Institute of Guidance Counsellors (1995). *Policy Statement on Training of Guidance Counsellors*, Dublin: Institute of Guidance Counsellors.

Jeffers, G. (2002). "The Re-structured Senior Cycle and the Guidance Counsellor", *Institute of Guidance Counsellors Journal*. Retrieved from: www.nuim.ie /academic/education/Adobe/sc-gc.pdf.

McCarthy, J. (1993). *The Vocational needs of Irish disadvantaged youth*, Study undertaken for CEDEFOP, Luxembourg: CEDEFOP.

McCoy, S., E. Smyth, M. Darmody and A. Dunne (2004). "Guidance Provision in Post-Primary Schools", International Guidance Conference, Dublin.

McCoy, S. (2004). "The Lifelong Implications of Guidance and Counselling at Second Level in Ireland", CEDEFOP Conference, Thessaloniki, October 2004.

McGuinness, S. (2001). *The Allocation of Teachers to Second Level Schools. Report of the Expert Group to the Minister for Education and Science.* http://www.irlgov.ie/educ/alloc

McKenna, P., G. McNamara and T. Barrett (1997). *Principals' Perceptions of the Guidance Service in Post-Primary Schools*, Dublin: National Centre for Guidance in Education.

National Centre for Guidance in Education (1996). *Guidelines for the Practice of Guidance and Counselling*, Dublin: National Centre for Guidance in Education.

National Centre for Guidance in Education (1997). *Careers Information Materials in Irish Schools*, Dublin: National Centre for Guidance in Education.

National Centre for Guidance in Education (1997). *Principals' Perceptions of the Guidance Service in Post-primary Schools*, Dublin: National Centre for Guidance in Education.

National Centre for Guidance in Education (1999). *Guidance Review*, Dublin: National Centre for Guidance in Education.

National Centre for Guidance in Education (1999). *Guidance and Counselling in Post-primary schools, pilot study*, Dublin: National Centre for Guidance in Education.

National Centre for Guidance in Education (2001). *Audit of Guidance and Counselling in Post-Primary Schools*, Dublin: National Centre for Guidance in Education.

National Centre for Guidance in Education (2004). *Planning the School Guidance Programme*, Dublin: National Centre for Guidance in Education.

NESF (2002). *Early School Leavers*, Dublin: NESF.

OECD (2002). *OECD Review of Career Guidance Policies, Ireland Country Note*, Paris: OECD.

OECD (2003). "Career Guidance: New Ways Forward" in *Education Policy Analysis 2003*, Paris: OECD.

OECD (2004). *Career Guidance and Public Policy. Bridging the Gap*, Paris: OECD.

O'Leary, E. (1990). "Research on school counselling: An Irish perspective", *The School Counselor*, Vol. 37, pp. 261-270.

Shiel, G. and M. Lewis (1993). "Guidance and Counselling in Irish Second-Level Schools", *The Irish Journal of Education*, Vol, 27, Nos. 1 and 2, pp. 5-24.

Smyth, E. and C. Hannan (2002). *Who Chooses Science? Subject Take-Up in Second-Level Schools*, Dublin: Economic and Social Research Institute in association with The Liffey Press.

Smyth, E., D. Byrne and C. Hannan (2004). *The Transition Year Programme: An Assessment*, Dublin: Economic and Social Research Institute in association with The Liffey Press.

Smyth, E., S. McCoy and M. Darmody (2004). *Moving Up: The Experiences of First Year Students in Post-Primary Education*, Dublin: Economic and Social Research Institute in association with The Liffey Press.

Smyth, E., A. Dunne, S. McCoy and M. Darmody (2006). *Pathways through the Junior Cycle*, Dublin: Economic and Social Research Institute in association with The Liffey Press.

Sultana, R. (2004). *Guidance Policies in the Knowledge Society. Trends, challenges and responses across Europe.* Office for Official Publications of the European Communities, Luxembourg, Cedefop Panorama Series 85.

Watts, A. G. and R.G. Sultana (2003). "Career Guidance Policies in 36 countries: Contrasts and Common Themes"'. A paper commissioned by CEDEFOP for a conference of Career Guidance and Public Policy: Bridging the Gap, Toronto, Canada, www.igc-edu.ie/megasynthesis.htm